Cosmic Astrology

June Wakefield

ISBN-10: 0-86690-250-3
ISBN-13: 978-0-86690-250-2

Cover Design: Jack Cipolla

Published by:
American Federation of Astrologers, Inc.
6535 S. Rural Road
Tempe, AZ 85283

www.astrologers.com

Printed in the United States of America

CONTENTS

Introduction

Cosmic astrology, as known and lived by the ancients, pointed the way of man's journey in life through the ages of time. If it were correctly understood and used today it would also point the way for man's regeneration and return to Pure Source, the Godhead from which humanity, and all life comes. This ancient knowledge lives; it can never be destroyed. Words of truth live forever, but humanity in the endless striving for wealth and power pushes them into the background to be seemingly lost, to lie forgotten, except by a very few of the truly advanced sages who will keep them alive until mankind wearies of warring with his brother and exploiting for gain against those weaker than himself.

These old teachings of wisdom can be found if one cares to seek. They are in the Bible, the Kabala, the Chaldean Book of Numbers, the Stanzas of Dzyan and in old mythology. The meanings are always obscured and difficult to understand, but they are there. They are recorded in the Mystery Schools; the pyramids, and in the still undeciphered rock libraries of Sumer and many other lands. No one can as yet say where it came from originally, but tradition traces it as coming from Atlantis with the fleeing populace at the time of the last great cataclysm and the final sinking of the island.

Our only interest at this time is in seeking out the true meanings hidden in astrology. We are flooded with books giving good step-by-step instruction for making the chart. What you will learn here will show you the way to correctly understand that chart.

Our first consideration will be to attempt to give a true understanding of the spiritual background of astrology, and how closely entwined religion and astrology are and have always been, since the beginning of man on earth. These abstract principles will be covered to the best of our ability in chapter three, which is devoted to spiritual astrology.

Actually this book is not written for the beginner in astrology, for we will not attempt to explain the terms used. To do so would take too much time and space away from the message we wish to give you-the message of the sacred meaning to be found in astrology. However, I believe this book will be of inestimable value for those who have an interest in astrology but cannot accept the contradictions to be found in the present day system.

We are going to devote our energies to a thorough understanding of the nature of each planet, what they really are and what influence they have upon earth and the people of earth. We will study the zodiacal signs and discover the pattern of their work. We will learn the way each planet functions through a male and a female sign. We will come to appreciate the exact pattern under which each operates, and understand the law of the universe which decrees to the second the precise location of each planet for thousands of years in advance as each moves in its allotted place in the heavenly spheres. If we keep in mind the fact that what we have here on earth and in our solar system is duplicated many thousands of times over, out in interstellar space, we may even come to realize in a limited way the magnitude of the universe in which we live.

Medical science now acknowledges that the moon has a definite effect upon mental illness. Surgeons admit that the phases of the moon have a relationship to the amount of bleeding following surgery, hemorrhaging being a greater danger at the time of the full moon. This corresponds to the fact that the moon controls the tides. As the moon controls the fluids of the earth, so does it also control the fluids of man's physical body. Why do we question that there must also be an influence from the other planets?

Although it is contrary to popular conception because of ignorance of the deeper meanings, astrology is a science. It is not a pseudo-science, nor is it an exploded theory as is believed by many. Astrology is totally unknown in its true form. Sometime in the not too far distant future the hidden wisdom of the old astrology will be recognized, and a "new" science will find its way into our universities. All the misconceptions and the misunderstandings of ages past will have to be sheared away to make way for the more enlightened knowledge. It is my ambition and my hope in writing this book to help clear the way. I have no interest in trying to sell astrology to the unbelievers. I hope to give to those who seek the answers the benefit of many years of concentrated study, and to show by very reasonable and logical concepts that astrology must be moved out of the realm of entertainment and superstition and into its rightful place among the serious studies.

I want to specify at the start that I consider this book to be but a mere beginning—a mere drop in the bucket compared to the work that lies ahead. This will I hope be a stepping stone for future findings. My teacher has students in all parts of the world who will recognize her teachings. It is my earnest wish that one of them will carry on from where I leave off, and fill the many loopholes that I must leave unfilled. There are so many answers I do not know. There will be so much that will be unfinished, but what I have put down as true I am fully convinced in my own mind is true. I am convinced that my teacher's revelation is a portion of the old, forgotten, "lost" wisdom of the ages. It is the basis, the very foundation of all the religions of the earth, the sciences, the principles by which man lives. And so we continue to seek. A Master promised "seek and ye shall find," but we were not promised easy going.

June Wakefield

CHAPTER I

WHAT ASTROLOGY IS AND IS NOT

For many years a popular misconception of astrology has persisted: the belief that astrology is only an art of prediction, that it has no other value to man other than that of peering into the future. Few realize that it has been of relatively recent times that it has become so perverted and its pristine beauty so deeply tarnished by using it solely as a method of entertainment. True, there is much value even in this if the chart is correctly interpreted, but it is a mistake to suppose that this is its sole value.

Astrology was the religion of the ancients. We must make clear, however, just what we mean when we speak of the ancients. We are not speaking of the astrologers or the mystics of the Dark Ages, nor of those who practiced around the beginning of Christianity on earth. No, when we speak of the ancients we are referring to those wise scholars who understood and sought to preserve the pure and sacred meaning of astrology in the time before the Biblical era and during the time of the Old Testament. Astrology was the science as well as the religion of those past ages. At some time in the future it will become the bridge of understanding that draws together science and religion once again. Of recent years it has been pooh-poohed as a pseudoscience, a parlor game, a fun thing that no one in his right mind would take seriously. Yet it has lived through the ages. History records it at the time of the Babylonians and the Chaldeans. Occult tradition traces it back much further. It has flourished in China, in Persia, in India, among the learned and the wise as well as among the naive and the ignorant. There is enough truth in it to convince the thoughtful person that there must be a basis of fact, and enough nonsense to convince the skeptical one that. it is all humbug. There is much that is true in modern astrology as practiced today. There is even more that is in error. One bright and shining fact stands forth, however: the constant search. Very few are really satisfied with astrology as it stands today. The search goes on, for everyone instinctively knows that so much more has once existed and been lost in time. Even those who make their living by duping the gullible change their concepts from time to time. One school calls their teachings The New Astrology. There is no such thing as a *new* astrology. It is as old as time and it antedates humanity on the physical plane. It was the religion of Earth's first people, those ethereal beings who "walked with God and talked with God, and were instructed by angelic intelligences," as told to us by ancient scriptures.

Astrologers of today know that a precise and perfect mathematical pattern is missing. And they know that such a pattern has to exist in this precise and perfect mathematical universe. Some controversy still exists as to which signs are governed by which planets, and changes have been made—arbitrary attempts to take from one planet a sign and give it to another. Thus have modern astrologers with their guessing and their changing ideas done much to destroy all that is logical and beneficial in the ancient wisdom of cosmic astrology—those spiritual, abstract principles that are represented by those heavenly bodies, the planets, and the signs through which they function.

It is only fair to state, however, that the astrologers of this day are becoming aware that there are deeper meanings, more spiritual wisdom hidden in astrology than has been discovered up to the present time, and they are trying to find the answers that have proven puzzling. What my teacher discovered in more than half a lifetime of intense study is hereby laid before you, and I feel that this could well be the breakthrough, the initial step away from superstition and foolishness and toward the fullest and deepest religious concepts of this ancient religion of the stars.

Astrology is not basically an art of prediction, although it can be used as such with a great deal more accuracy than shown in the present system. Its value lies in an understanding of the deep and fundamental meanings of life and of mankind which the student gains as he or she correctly understands the concepts. It gives an objective knowledge of the material universe in which we live, for we cannot study the movements of the sun with its family of planets, the solar system in its place in the galaxy, and the galaxy itself without becoming aware of a Great Intelligence governing these movements, and coming to a firm conviction that the entire universe is governed by law and order. Nothing happens by chance.

This is not a study to be undertaken lightly. Nor can its principles be grasped in a few days of idle investigation. It can be comprehended only by thorough study and deep meditation, allowing the abstract principles to become a part of one's consciousness.

Astrology and the natal chart will not tell one the plane on which he or she is functioning, nor will it tell the degree of spiritual development that has been attained. A seer, or the greatest of intellectual giants will have the exact same chart as will a puppy if they happen to be born at the same time and the same place. True, the puppy may have an unusual degree of intelligence, but that intelligence will be strictly on a puppy level. The way a man or woman responds to the happenings in his life, what he she does with his or her talents and abilities, tells his or her place in evolution and the degree of advancement.

Astrology was never meant to provide one with a ready-made alibi. Our horoscopes will show the strengths and the apparent weaknesses to be found in each planet or sign, as well as the influence shed by each planet's position in relation to every other planet, which are called the aspects. We have stressed the word "apparent" here because a weakness is not within the planet or the sign, but within ourselves. Therefore, it only appears to be a weakness or even a malignant influence from the heavenly body. Our very human faults and weaknesses do show up, and it is much more convenient to place the blame some other place than upon ourselves; nevertheless, that is one of the greatest values of astrology: finding where we can improve ourselves. To use astrology to excuse our own failings and drift along putting forth no effort to improve is profaning a sacred art.

Our charts will also show us which departments of life will have the most activity, and those that will need special care. These are called the mundane houses, and tell quite a story when we learn to read them.

It is interesting to note how many people do find an excuse for their failure to make the best of their opportunities. It is not always comfortable to face up to the fact that we do have free will, and do, to a large extent, determine what events come to us.

One woman I know has Uranus in the first house, close to the Ascendant. She commented, "You see? I just can't help being restless. I have to keep moving and changing." I was most sympathetic and thought how very sad to be the victim of a force that one cannot control. This was at the very beginning of my interest in astrology. Soon, however, I discovered that my teacher also has Uranus in the first house, and even closer to the Ascendant. The contrast between her useful and interesting activities and the other woman's aimless drifting were, to say the least, a revelation to me. The first one folded her hands helplessly, bewailing her hard luck, sighing in self pity, wasting her talents. She was satisfied to blame a force outside herself for her failures. My teacher looked about her for something constructive to do. She found so much of such absorbing interest that her long life has been full to overflowing with happiness and activity. She is an inspiration to all who know her, and her friends are legion.

So, above all, astrology is not a doctrine of fatalism. It points out the gifts we are born with, our abilities, our assignments in this lifetime, what we are to accomplish here and now. If we fail these assignments we forge a chain which will continue to draw us back again and again until we do complete our work for humanity, and for our own soul's development.

A natal chart is a blueprint, a chart of the heavens at the moment we draw into our bodies our first breath of life, and so impress upon our souls and bodies the position of the planetary forces, the signs they are functioning through, and the houses (departments of life) in which they will be most active. The planets and the signs they are functioning through show us our potential talents, our main interest in life and our relationship to humanity as a whole. The aspects between these planets indicate where we will encounter obstacles and problems, or the lucky break that will help us over a rough spot. The mundane houses show the department of life where these activities will take place.

We could consider the natal chart to be a book of instructions that accompany every newborn baby, printed in heavenly realms to help and assist him or her on the journey through life. We are not trying to say that once the blueprint is impressed within us our whole future is preordained; to do so would remove our most precious gift, that of free will. God and the Cosmic Masters do not interfere in our wayward wanderings. We choose our own path. If we err we have to pay the price for our mistakes. We are right now making payment on the mistakes of the past, a past life. This would indicate a difficult chart. If this is shown in a horoscope it is possible to turn aside, or at least soften somewhat, the penalty by sincere prayer, meditation and good works toward our fellow man. This cannot always be accomplished as sometimes our fault has been of such a nature that no other way would be effective save that of suffering. Nevertheless, many problems can be averted. We can never rule our stars, but we can and must rule our reaction to their influences. We win or lose by the way we respond to planetary vibrations.

Your book of instructions shows you only what you should do, it does not force you to follow instructions. If you choose to waste your talents and potentials rather than develop them you are free to do so, but do not blame the stars for the ill fortune that you, and you alone attract into your life. We must not lose sight of the fact, either, that the way we are living our life in this cycle determines the chart we will be bringing with us into the next.

We are like radio receiving sets; the vibrations are broadcast from the heavens as from a giant broadcasting station out in interstellar space. We receive them and send them forth into the region about us. Being, as we are, such faulty instruments, we are apt to broadcast static rather than heavenly music. We may receive beautiful music, but in attempting to send it on we respond to the force of the vibrations in a purely human way and thereby lay up untold problems for ourselves. Take for instance the energy of Mars; it is a vital influence in our lives, but the way we react to that energy is all-important. An unevolved Mars personality reacts with anger and thoughts of revenge to a wrong done him, but a Mars personality who has learned through experience the futility of revenge, the self-destructive quality of anger, will set about forcibly to set things straight. Energy is still used, but in a way that accomplishes the desired end, thereby showing the high evolutionary status of the person using that Mars energy.

One of the most unfortunate mistakes of some of the modern astrologers is the habit of referring to Mars and Saturn as the Lesser and the Greater Malefics, indicating that they exert an evil influence in our lives. Ancient astrology with its sublime, abstract principles tells us that every planet is an attribute of God. There can be no evil planets nor malefic influences from them, for there is no evil from God. The evil and suffering is of our own making, due entirely to our wrong responses to the vibratory influences.

Every planet in the heavens (in our own solar system exclusively) has a center in our physical body. For instance, the sun is the cosmic heart and has its corresponding center in the human heart. So it is with every planet. These centers exist within us and we all respond to them and the urges they receive according to our state of progress and enlightenment. There will be more on these centers and the urges they receive in the chapter on the planets.

Ancient astrology is vast in scope, completely understandable, and harmonious to science, religion, and the secret mystery teachings. It relates to Greek and Roman mythology and to the myths and traditions of all lands. Once an understanding is attained it forms a link bridging the known and the unknown. The farther back we go into antiquity the more pure and perfect we find the science of astrology. It has gone through idolatry, Phallic worship and general mutilation. Down through the ages it has been changed by the people of that time into what they wanted it to be and to do for them, but it could never be destroyed.

Astrology is an ancient wisdom. Wisdom differs from knowledge inasmuch as knowledge is acquired from books and other sources. Wisdom is the result, coming from within, a combination of study and deep inner meditation. It then becomes a part of our consciousness, available for our use. Knowledge, however, has to be memorized, and the facts sorted and then accepted or rejected. Once knowledge becomes wisdom, it becomes a part of us, readily available.

Astrology is a science of the heavens. It shows us what we are, what our work in this life should be, the lessons we have to learn in order to become like our prototype, the Heavenly Man, or Supernal Being, to become the image of the Son, as the Son is the Image of the Father. The Greeks called this perfected Image in man the Christos, or Christ. To bring forth the Christ in every man is the ultimate goal of humanity. Astrology charts the path.

As the Monad, that eternal being inhuman form, journeys through the rounds of evolution, the only way possible for him to gain wisdom and purification is through experiences while in the flesh, living earthly lives. The periods between lives are for the purpose of assimilating and absorbing into the very core of our beings all the lessons learned while alive and on earth. Since we only learn by doing, the ancients never considered an evil act against our fellow man as a sin, but rather as a regrettable mistake that one must correct. They knew that retribution would have to be made, but the offender was never condemned nor harshly judged. They knew that each of us must learn from our own mistakes, and they also knew that "the mills of the gods grind slowly, but they grind exceedingly small."

The events in our lives are not so important as is the way we react to them. For instance, let us consider the chart of a criminal. Astrologers will take the chart of a Hitler or another person who has committed all kinds of atrocities and proceed to analyze this "evil" chart, finding all kinds of "evil" planets, signs, and aspects. They ignore completely the fact that thousands of other humans were born at exactly the same moment, but according to their different reactions, of their own choosing, led totally different lives. Many of them were outstandingly useful and happy. The same planetary influences were in their charts, the same signs and aspects, but they used their gift of free will and chose the better life. Thus we can be inspired to lift ourselves up to a better life now. In doing so we also pave the way for a brighter life on our next trip into this earthly sphere.

The doctrine of reincarnation is easy to accept when looked at in this light: life is a succession of lessons that must be lived to be understood. One lifetime could never be enough to reach perfection, and without reaching perfection what would be the purpose behind life at all? When we consider a series of lives, much as a child passing through a series of school terms with vacation periods free of lessons but assimilating the lessons formerly learned, life has more meaning and death loses its sting. Children begin their education at kindergarten level. We begin our physical lives as primitive people and progress as best we can, by trial and error, to repeat them until we do learn the lessons and the particular lessons that we have failed to grasp.

I have no interest whatever in converting anyone to a belief in reincarnation. If you have an interest in the subject but wonder why there is no reference to it by that name in the Bible, I suggest you research for yourself the history of the Ecumenical Councils that have been in progress from time to time since the early Christian era, and see how the minds of man have tampered with and changed sacred scriptures for their own purposes. They have come up with some truly strange conclusions. For instance, at one early Council the learned Church Fathers, those who arbitrarily decided the fundamental doctrines and dogmas of the church, debated many days over the weighty question of whether women had souls. The decision was that they did not! At the same time those wise and learned leaders of men removed the female principle from the Trinity. Instead of Father and Mother producing the Son, it became, through human decree, Father and Son, two male qualities, producing the Holy Ghost.

With astrology showing us our assignments in life we can leap ahead of the ordained evolutionary period by virtue of our individual efforts. Our progress is ordained only in the sense of averages. We may fall behind or surge ahead of the masses, according to the amount of effort we are willing to put forth in gaining knowledge, and the amount of truly unselfish work we are willing to do in helping others. Every time we accept a helping hand we have incurred a debt to the cosmic which can be dispelled only by turning to give a helping hand to the brother on the path behind us.

Summary

1. Astrology is a study of the heavens, the movement of heavenly bodies and the influence they exert upon the lives and affairs of humanity.

2. The higher use of astrology was never that of predicting the future.

3. Everything in the entire universe, including man, is governed by exact and perfect laws.

4. Realization comes to us via these studies that we are not victims of a capricious fate, but meet in this life the results of past lives, and that we forge our future lives by the way we live this one.

5. Astrology does not give us an alibi for our shortcomings. The planetary vibrations are an influence to which we respond according to our individual plane of development. When we cooperate, our path is easier and our progress—spiritual, mental, and material—is hastened.

6. Our horoscope is the blueprint of our own soul and a map of our assignments for this life. The soul-pattern of the individual is in the life seed, and unfolds what has been infolded in the seed.

7. Our lives are not foreordained except in a general trend. We have free will to err but must pay the price of our willful ways.

8. There can be no evil from the heavens. Whatever evil there be in our lives is a result of our own actions and created within ourselves, not sent from above.

CHAPTER 2

HISTORY OF ASTROLOGY

The Chaldeans (a priestly cult of Babylonia) have been credited with first observing the influence of the planets in our lives, events, and the evolution of earth and its people. They are responsible for bringing it forth in its relatively modern form; that is, the art of predicting the future. The deeper meanings go far back into antiquity, back to the Golden Age and the history of man's beginnings in physical form.

During the Golden Age it was constant summer for thousands of years as the climate all over the earth was tropical. There was no struggle for existence, for the good Mother Earth had substance in plenty for all. Time was devoted to spiritual interests. Astrology was the religion of that day, and people lived their lives according to its precepts, seeing in it the laws of nature and the light of God. It is said of that time that "men walked with God and talked with God, and were instructed by angelic intelligences." Certainly no human mind brought forth this most ancient of religions, the religion of the stars.

When the tipping of the axis occurred, putting an end to the Golden Age, earth was inclined in such a way that the sun could no longer shine upon all portions of the earth at the same time and the once tropical land became frozen. Most of the people who survived became meat eaters and nomads moving from place to place. Only a few of the very advanced kept alive the sacred teachings in the form of stories and parables, which down through the ages have become myths. The myths of all lands are so similar that they show beyond reasonable doubt that all lands and all people have this common origin. They also show that all peoples had a belief in the influence of the heavenly bodies in their affairs and looked to them for guidance and inspiration.

The Religion of the Stars, now known as astrology, could not therefore have originated with the Chaldeans. It has existed since time began. It is said that it was taught to early humanity by spiritual intelligences at some time during prehistorical ages. It was not only a religion but an exact science of the heavens and included all the other sciences pertaining to earth. It had remained unaltered for thousands of years until a later humanity had forgotten its history and also had lost the ability to understand its religious meanings as well as its sciences and the many other sciences contained within it.

The early humanity was gone. Those with the perfect understanding and their descendants had been sinking deeper and deeper into a spiritual and mental atmosphere of darkness for many thousands of years, a veritable midnight of ignorance and superstition. They were an unhappy people; they knew they had lost a spiritual value. In their struggle to find some way out of their darkness they invented one religion after another. And so it continues to the present time.

If will be of benefit now to take a backward look to the time in history when Sumer, in what was later known as Mesopotamia, was a flourishing community of highly cultured people. Occult science places the time of the settling of Sumer a few years before the final devastation that resulted in the sinking of Atlantis. Colonizing had been going on for ages. At the time of the last great flood and final destruction there were already colonies established in many places for the fleeing populace if they succeeded in escaping.

Sumer was one of those places. Those who reached safety there brought with them the science and culture of their homeland. They lived there in peace for no one knows how long, but eventually they were taken over by the Babylonians. Their rich stores of knowledge were confiscated, and astrology, along with the other sciences, fell into the hands of a people who were unable to grasp the deeper spiritual meanings. It was a new science to them, this strange religion of the stars, but they could see that it worked for the Sumerians in all ways in their daily living, and they attempted to put it to work for themselves. Their outlook upon life was too materialistic and their understanding too limited for them to comprehend the religious concepts of a more spiritually advanced people. This is when the Chaldean soothsayers acquired it and converted it into an art of prediction. It then lost its meaning and value, both as a religion and a science, and remained only a device for common fortune telling. There is still a degree of accuracy, but down through the ages there has been change after change until now very little remains of the original teachings.

Until about the end of the nineteenth century, Sumer had been looked upon as a mythical land. There was no evidence to prove that such a people had ever existed. In 1877, the French began the first successful excavation in what is now Mesopotamia, but was formerly known as Sumer. This was followed ten years later by an American expedition under John P. Peters, a professor of Hebrew at the University of Pennsylvania. The origin of the people of Sumer has never been completely established, but it is known that they were neither of Semitic nor Indo-European origin. Although it remains a mystery to archeologists, legend and tradition claim the Atlantean exodus as populating the area of Sumer. The time of their residency is given as from the beginning of the fourth to the end of the third millennium BC. Huge libraries written in cuneiform have been unearthed and are being deciphered. Here are found many of the ancient myths, epics, hymns, and stories. Who knows what interesting facts will be brought to light as this excavation work goes on?

The pagan priesthood of Chaldea knew that this had been a world religion at one time that was based upon the movement of the stars and other heavenly bodies, and they knew astronomy pretty well. They set out to change the science of astrology to fit the times in which they lived, which certainly had changed greatly in later centuries. Not only had the intelligence level of the people in general become very low but their moral level had fallen even lower due to the intellectual darkness which was settling over the world.

The history of this time of darkness is in the Bible. Read Genesis 19, and many other chapters of the Old Testament. The story of the degeneracy of that day is there. The Chaldean priests apparently did not know about the Inner Universe, and the heavenly or supernal man, the Image, in the likeness of which earth-man was created and of which he is the reflection.

Among the Initiates, those of enlightened wisdom, these ancient and sacred teachings have always been referred to as the Written Law and the Oral Law. Of the Written Law, or astrology, it was said that the laws of the manifested Universe were written in characters of Light in the stars. It was called the Golden Key. The Oral Law was passed from teacher to pupil orally and was never put into written words. This was known as the Silver Key.

The Oral Law contained the inner meanings and spiritual interpretations of astrology and had to be committed to memory. No notes were allowed except as a system of symbology was devised and each pupil was allowed to record that day's teachings upon a card in symbols whose meanings were known only to Initiates. These became known as the tarot cards. Were it possible to find these cards today in their original form we would have the entire story of creation in pictograph as well as the whole beautiful story of the evolution of man, earth, and the universe.

However, these cards have also passed through many hands and their sacred teachings changed by men who have tried to explain them. The Silver Key has become tarnished, but the pure silver, the sacred meanings, still lie concealed under the tarnish of the ages and will be found again when the time is right. The superstitions, wrong understanding, and the accumulated tarnish of the ages will be removed and the Silver Key found to gleam as brightly as before. When this takes place the Golden Key will also be found to be as pure and perfect as in the days of old when these two—Golden Key and Silver Key—were used together to guide man's destiny.

It will be a note of interest here to state that the tarot cards fell into the hands of roving bands of nomads known as Gypsies who claim Egypt as their land of origin. It 6is highly probable that it was in Egypt that these cards first carne into their possession. For generations the ancient wisdom has been safeguarded by these people who had not the slightest idea of the treasure they held in their hands. Possibly some of the more advanced among them did recognize a beauty and a truth beyond their understanding, for they kept the cards in a near likeness to the originals. They had no other use for these cards than that of profit and entertainment. They added the fifty-six cards of the Minor Arcana to the twenty-two original, known as the Major Arcana, to enlarge and embellish the entertainment they offered to the public as fortune telling.

As the bands of Gypsies roamed through other countries, the peoples of those lands adopted the cards, changing them to suit themselves, until they too lost all semblance to the originals and the truth they contained. I know of only one near-replica that has retained the original symbology, and that is not to be had in card form. They have been reproduced in an old book by Count Saint Germain that has long been out of print.

As the cards passed through many hands and nations, they lost much of the value of even predicting the future, keeping only the germ of truth, barely enough to keep it alive. To me it is highly significant, however, that even that much has survived. Words of truth do not die. They live forever.

Perhaps the richest source of ancient wisdom relative to the old astrology is to be found in the Stanzas of Dzyan as they are analyzed and explained in *The Secret Doctrine* by Helena Blavatsky. This manuscript, the Stanzas of Dzyan, is a very old book written in Senzar; there is only one known original copy now in existence. Ir is the original work from which the oldest religious books of all nations have been compiled. The oldest Hebrew book of occult learning, *The Book of Concealed Mysteries*, China's primitive Bible, *the Chaldean Book of Numbers*, India's Puranas, and the first five books of our own Bible, the *Pentateuch*.

The Stanzas describe the forming of the universe, the evolution of the earth and the history of the races from the beginning of man on earth right down to us, the fifth race in the middle of the fourth round. It ends its history there, more than five thousand years ago. All of these old books contain some portion of this old science-religion. It is not ready made for any of us. Much effort and years of work go into that type of research, but that which is given to us without any effort on our part is rarely appreciated. Work and effort on our part is necessary. The *Kabala*, sacred book of the Jews, confirms and clarifies these ancient teachings.

So these old teachings are not lost; they do exist today. When the world is ready they will again be publicized and their rich, inspirational message will be given to the masses. This cannot be until humanity as a whole realizes the futility of wars and hatred, until we can live at peace with our neighbor. They can be found by the individual seeker, however, just as we are finding them, if we are willing to persist and by our efforts prove our worthiness to receive them.

Carvings found on temple walls, in caves, and on rocks in all parts of the world depict a common origin of the peoples of the world. The same myths, stories, and traditions exist among them all. These carvings show that a thorough understanding of the nature of the planets and the zodiacal signs was a part of the lives of the people of antiquity in North and South America as well as in Europe, Asia, and Africa. The South Sea Islands, and especially the Easter Isles, are rich in carvings denoting the same beliefs. Ivar Lissner has written of archaeological findings in some most fascinating books. James Churchward, in his books about the lost continent of Ma, or Lemuria, shows with photographs and drawings of old inscriptions that the people of that old, old land had as a basis for their beliefs in their religion a firm belief in the true form of cosmic astrology.

Pharaoh Amenhotep IV, during the eighteenth dynasty in Egypt, tried to bring back to his people a worship of the one God instead of the many gods worshiped by his people. He was called a sun-worshiper for his efforts. Neither he nor his people worshiped the sun, but they did worship the Invisible Sun with the sun as the visible symbol. The priesthood had too strong a hold on the people of that time for a concept of this kind to be accepted. Man was not yet ready to do his own thinking. Even today we are apt to cling to that which is familiar and let someone else worry about "new" ideas. It is so much easier to believe than it is to think. We must consider new information, however, if we wish to progress, retaining that which seems right to us and laying the rest aside for future consideration. That which we may now accept has only a relative reality which we discard as we reach a higher plane of development.

At about the time that Amenhotep IV passed from his plane of action there was a writer of books, a sage with vast mystical knowledge know as Hermes. He was born in Thebes in about 1399 BC and died in 1257 BC at the age of one hundred and forty-two years. His mummy lies in a cachette in the vicinity of El Amarna, Egypt. So great and legendary was his learning that he is often confused with the legends of the Egyptian god Thoth, the personification of universal wisdom. As late as 363 AD, the priests of Egypt had forty-two books which they attributed to Hermes. Of these, thirty-six contained the history of all human knowledge: science, astrology, religion, and medical.

The Astor Library in New York has a facsimile of an Egyptian treatise that is believed by authorities to be one of the six *Hermetic Books of Medicine*. It is known as the *Papyrus Ebers*. Formerly it had been believed that all forty-two books of Hermes had been burned at the holocaust of Alexandria; at least they all disappeared. Now, with the supposed appearance of one of the medical books, hope is revived that others will appear. It is not known how many other books were included among the Books of Hermes, but it is believed that they record the spiritual as well as the material progress of man since his advent upon earth.

There are ancient records that have been removed from our Bible that are known as the *Book of Enoch*, which contain chapters called *The Book of the Heavenly Luminaries*. I have seen reference to this many times but have not been able to find many concrete facts about it. Finally, I did find a book by Cannon Charles with parts of *The Book of the Heavenly Luminaries* in it. I found them to be confirmative rather than explanatory, but the very fact that it has been published is vastly encouraging as it shows a revival of interest in the old teachings.

In Manly P. Hall's book, *The Story of Astrology*, he quotes Cicero as saying that the Chaldeans had records of the stars for a space of 370,000 years. Greek writers credited Babylonians with like records for hundreds of thousands of years. "Even rejecting such fabulous statements," says Mr. Hall, "what boasted science of the moderns can be said to be built upon a more substantial foundation?" Mr. Hall further states that "the ancient astrologers were wiser than their modern imitators."

The Arabians called astrology the mother of sciences. The Hindus, are the oldest surviving nation, and astrology is their oldest science. It was practiced in India thousands of years before the Vedas were compiled. Dante called astrology the noblest of sciences. Confucius also was acquainted with astrology and wrote that "good and evil do not wrongly befall men, but heaven sends down misery or happiness according to their conduct."

So these teachings are far from new. To speak of a new astrology is but to say that once again that feeble man is attempting to impose his own puny intellect upon sublime words of truth. I doubt if man is qualified to change or improve Divine principles.

In this new Aquarian Age much more will be brought to light. Universal welfare can advance only according to individual effort and progress. May these sacred truths, gleaned so painstakingly and shared so willingly by my teacher, point the way and light the path to a higher understanding.

Summary
1. Astrology did not start in Chaldea, but the art of prediction did have its beginning there. The origin of astrology has been lost in time, although we find that it existed as far back in time as anything can be traced.

2. Occult tradition traces the science-religion—astrology—from Lemuria through Atlantis and into Sumer.

3. The Chaldean priesthood attempted to use the new-found science after Sumer was conquered, but they only succeeded in converting it into an art of prediction.

4. That astrology was the universal world religion can hardly be doubted when we know that astrological symbols have been found in archaeological excavations in every country in the world.

5. The Gypsies, through the use of the tarot cards, have done much to keep the ancient truths alive.

6. The *Stanzas of Dzyan* and *The Secret Doctrine* are perhaps the most readily available sources of information relative to cosmic astrology, but the *Kabala* and other sources confirm it.

CHAPTER 3

THE SPIRITUAL NATURE OF ASTROLOGY

The Zohar, Book of Splendor, has been called the most important literary work of the *Kabala*. It is full of secret wisdom, but so skillfully hidden as to be very difficult for the layman to understand. It has been stated, however, that "the effect upon the soul is not at all dependent

upon it being materially understood." The soul expands when exposed to words of sublime truth, whether completely understood or not. Understanding comes later when we allow our thoughts to dwell in meditation upon the words and concepts, especially if we do so just before dropping off to sleep.

The Zohar teaches a doctrine of ten Sephiroth from Divine source. "God, as He is in Himself, prior to the creation of the world, is called the Formless, Infinite, Hidden God. Being Formless, He yet caused Himself to be apprehended in the ten Sephiroth or Divine attributes and in each to be perceived." This God of the Universe the Hebrews called Einsoph (or Ainsoph), the Limitless Light. He emanated from Himself gradually, unfolding attributes which were called Sephiroth. From these in time, as density increased toward materiality, came planets, evolving from within toward outer manifestation, and from spiritual through astral and etheric to the material forms of the planets as attributes of God.

The first to be emanated forth was the one most like the Father, the King. In other words, the one to be first emanated forth was the visible symbol, the solar sun. This was the first manifestation and correspondence on the plane of nature to the spiritual, Invisible Sun, Einsoph, and contains in potency all that the spiritual Sun contains, and will eventually express all. Next in power and importance are the three secondary suns, expressing three main qualities of the Deity-Love, Wisdom, and practical use or union. The sun expresses through the whole solar system; they express through planes. There are also the six lower Sephiroth, each expressing through one planet and its two signs. This accounts for the ten Sephiroth, all ten principles, and it includes our Earth, which the Kabala says is a very important planet and has this to say about it: "The spirit of the Earth is as much a creator in its own realm as is the spirit of the Sun. The two are twins, interchangeable in function when not acting as two in one."

We will be quoting from old scriptures arid ancient manuscripts from time to time to illustrate a point, or just to enjoy the sheer beauty of the words. We know of no better way to bring home to the reader the fact that these teachings are not new, that they are not mere theory that cannot be proved, for verification does exist. It can be found in more than one source. Many of these old writings are older than the Bible, and many of them are from the same source. These quotations should give a deeper understanding to what we are writing and also bring about a clearer understanding of the Bible. We suggest that you allow them to permeate your mind without trying for objective understanding. Just float along with them; understanding will come later.

As one "whose Center is everywhere and Whose circumference is nowhere" there is no way to satisfactorily illustrate the Great Creative Power known as Godhead. The ancients simply used this symbol in an attempt to suggest to their students the potency and grandeur of this Power.

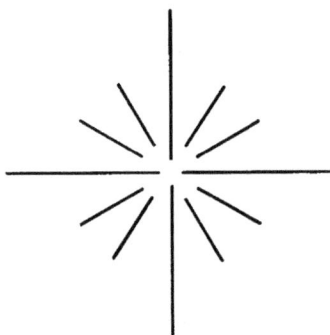

This part of our study will, I am sure, be the most difficult to master. Godhead, as Pure Spirit, can only be spiritually perceived, never scientifically explained. Spirit cannot be crystallized and high ideals and spiritual concepts lose the essence of their meaning when they try to become material facts through the use of words in our attempt to give expression to abstract values. Perhaps a direct quotation from the old sacred literature will make what is to follow a bit more clear. They said, "God projected a power of Himself into space, this gave rise to another, similar yet distinct, until ten projections had been established, like separate facets of one jewel."

Using tile illustration which we have just given we will now go further with a continuation of the same illustration but with much more added to it. We now attempt the impossible, that of putting into concrete words and form the abstract principles of cosmic astrology. The following can only be a two-dimensional illustration, not at all adequate or complete. We can only hope that it will suggest principles that some time spent in meditation will make clear. Allow intuition to take over now. Do not try to force objective comprehension; this will, in all probability, have to come later.

With the illustration before you now, observe that the celestial plane is the realm of Father-Mother, the One God, Supreme Ruler of the Universe. This is the Invisible Sun, Einsoph. There are the Four Spiritual Elements which surround the Godhead as a fog.

The spiritual plane is the invisible universe, potential space within abstract space. It is the inner invisible kingdom within the macrocosm, the Son or primordial and supernal man. It is the plane of spirit and soul, the ten Sephiroth as creative spiritual principles.

The material plane is interpenetrated with the astral and the etheric planes, all functioning together to complete a manifested universe, Nature. Strictly speaking, of course, manifestation is never completed but is a continuing process. This is the material reflection of the inner universe, its exact counterpart. It is the solar system containing the sun, the three secondary suns and the planets with their signs. This plane is also called Maya, the Great Illusion, in occult terminology. Here the ten Sephiroth as the Elohim, or Builders, get into action. The word Elohim has been translated as meaning "all the gods" or all the creative principles into material planetary form, the spiritual attributes of God.

The radiations of love and wisdom flow forth into all planes; the union of these radiations is the creative force of the Universe. From duality, when one expresses as two, a third is brought forth into being. This "law of the triangle" manifests on all plains. One is the undivided, potent, all-containing All. Two is the divided expression of the one. Three is the union or joining of these opposite expressions in order to create forms.

The exoteric (non-hidden) Kabalistic teachings speak of a central sun and three secondary suns in every solar system, our own included. The three secondary suns, each in its own orbit, revolve around the central solar sun. It will be noted that each secondary sun has under its rulership two planets that in turn work through two zodiacal signs. Each of these groups of four signs contain one sign of each element, two of which are male and two of which are female. Thus a perfect pattern is established. This will be increasingly apparent as we go along. At no time is there a lack of a perfect, precise, mathematical pattern. It has been said that abstract principles must lack proof, must be accepted on faith alone. In astrology there has been too much acceptance, too many theories, and too little proof. Too often those who command the largest vocabu-

Father - Mother

THE UNDIVIDED

THE ONE

Practicality

The All-Father
The Great Spirit

The Invisible Sun of Spirit
Einsoph, Limitless Light
Parabrahm

Inspiration

Aspiration

The Breakthrough

Emotion

LOVE

WISDOM

The Celestial Plane

Union
Holy Spirit
Fohat

Spiritual Plane

Material Plane interpenetrated
with the ethereal and the astral
planes.

♇   ⛢   ♆

♂   ♀   ⊕   ☽   ☿   ♃

♈ ♏ ♉ ♎ ♋ ♌ ♒ ♑ ♊ ♍ ♓ ♐

AIR
EARTH
WATER
FIRE

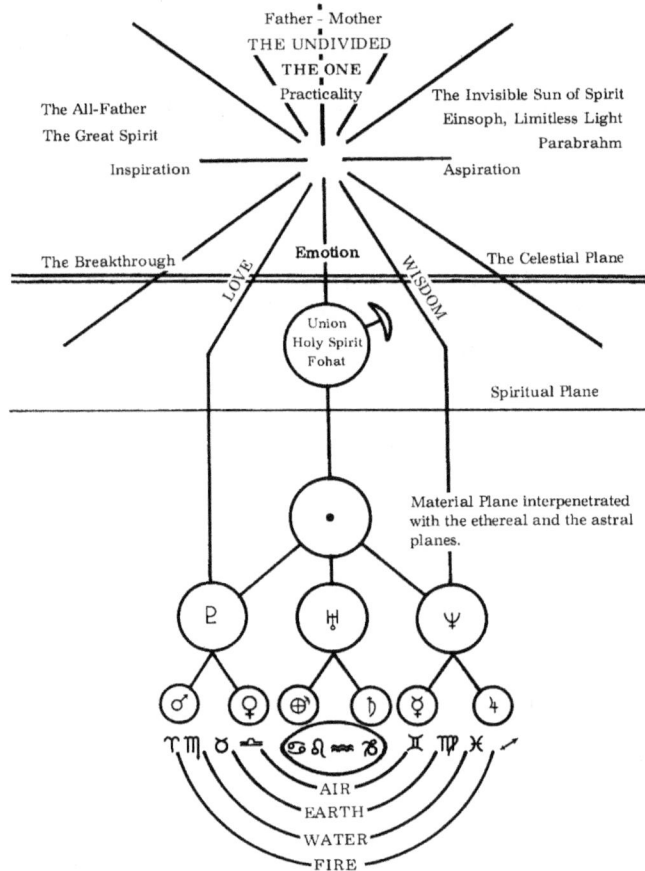

lary and the most persuasive manner of expression, whether there be the slightest element of truth in their teachings or not, have the greatest influence on the largest number of people. You will be able to see for yourself that cosmic astrology falls into the same pattern time after time, never having to be reconstructed to fit the pattern, nor the pattern changed to fit it.

Life precedes form. The symbol we see at the top of the illustration represents life before forms emerge, God's Pure Spirit, never changing, remaining forever invisible. Surrounding this Invisible Sun is an energy field composed of love and wisdom. From the center, waves come forth, growing denser as they travel away from their source. From *The Secret Doctrine* we learn "when the one becomes two, the third appears." The one has now separated into love (the Mother side of Deity) and wisdom (the Father side of Deity). Love and wisdom unite and form a third, unity or motion. This is the First Trinity, which produces the Son—the product—spiritual Universe—the kingdom within.

The Zohar tells us that before forms were created, signs were engraved in the energy field surrounding the Godhead and then divided into the four sacred elements. These four spiritual elements are carried over from the celestial realm into the spiritual realm and are called the Four Great Forces, the Sacred Four. Look again at the illustration, and realize that we are still speaking of the spiritual realm where nothing material exists, but the abstract principles or spiritual elements are active here as they are on all planes. They are not related to the material elements except as the material elements reflect the nature of the spiritual elements, which are inspiration, fire or life; emotion, water or soul; aspiration, air or mind; and practicality, earth or form. The spiritual elements are states of life on the inner plane which surrounds the Godhead. Their influence corresponds to the material elements but pertains to the Godhead.

All substances are brought forth from these Four Great Forces, or spiritual elements. From inspiration (or fire) comes spiritual substance; from emotion (water) comes astral substance; from aspiration (air) comes etherical substance; and from practicality (earth) comes material. substance.

When motion began within space, when eternal breath stirred within the boundless deep, or as the Bible puts it, "the Spirit of God moved upon the face of the Waters," waves of energy came forth from the innermost center moving outward. These must not be thought of as material waves for nothing was material as yet. They were spiritual radiations which, as they moved outward after eons of time and through the process of evolution, become material manifestations.

We have now reached the plane of beginning manifestation. Before the sun becomes visible, it goes through several stages: spiritual light, astral light, etherical light, and finally, material light. On the astral plane there is only the essence of matter, nothing fully material as yet. The three secondary suns are gradually forming, gradually evolving, each becoming active in its own plane. The solar sun contains all that the Invisible Sun contains, but in a densified form. The secondary suns also contain all; here, however, division occurs and each receives that radiation or cosmic substance peculiar to its own nature and to the plane of life governed by it. This is held as in a giant reservoir ready for distribution to the worker planets. From these secondary suns flows substance with which the worker planets function through the zodiacal signs.

Now the universe had become visible. This is the macrocosm, the material body of God, also called the supernal, or Heavenly Man. Although the universe had become visible, it was not complete. It is never a static creation nor finished. It is at all times evolving, eternally being perfected. It is like a newly born baby who is a finished product of the human race but still must constantly strive to develop and perfect himself according to the laws of God and nature.

We hear this material universe spoken of as a mechanism, but in reality it is an organism, composed of living, functioning organs. The visible universe is an exact replica of the invisible universe. "As above so below" is the premise upon which all wisdom teachings are based. Everything that exists in the macrocosm also exists in the microcosm, man. Micro means little, cosm is the cosmos, so many is a little cosmos. We will return to a further exploration of the nature of man in the following chapter.

Within and beyond the Universe is the Limitless Light whose rays constitute life, the life of the Universe, and all within. If you were asked to define life, what would you say? I have heard it defined as "the Essence of God Himself that energizes all things," and I have found no other definition so comprehensive, simple yet profound. The flows of love and wisdom streaming forth from the Godhead are always trying to find their way back together again to reunite. Through every plane they radiate toward each other. As the radiations meet and merge, that unity becomes the masculine-feminine creative force of the Universe. "one becomes two, and both produce three, and thee produce all things."

We find it active on all planes, the male and female seeking each other to unite and produce. This is the first law of nature. In the terminology of the ancients this dual creative force was called Fohat, the fiery whirlwind. It was also called the Holy Spirit, Holy Ghost, Spirit of Life, and the Logos. It is potential creative power as well as active creative power, depending upon the plane within which it is working.

Fohat is one thing in the unmanifested Universe and another in the manifested Universe. In the unmanifested Universe, Fohat is an abstract, philosophical idea, potential creative power. In the manifested Universe, it is that occult, electric, vital power that, under the will and direction of Elohim (the builders) unites and brings together all forms.

The Secret Doctrine says that Fohat is the cosmic, creative energy hissing through space; our scientists say that matter is being pounded into form in interstellar space and that thee is a hissing sound accompanying this action. There is really not so much difference in the two sciences as sometimes appears. The ancients said "Fohat hisses as he glides hither and thither" and represents him as a serpent with the head of a man.

In their picturesque way the ancients spoke of Fohat as an entity, almost as a playful personality cavorting about collecting the cosmic dust and rolling it into balls. "How does Fohat build them (the planetary chains)? He collects the fiery dust, he makes balls of fire, he runs through them, infusing them with life therein, and then sets them in motion, some one and some the other way." One wonders about this quotation. Could it possibly mean that although the worker planets spin on their axis in a counterclockwise direction, some of the others may not do the same? In *Astronomy Made Simple*, it is stated that Uranus revolves on its axis in a clockwise direction.

Fohat, or union, works on all planes. It is the essence of cosmic electricity, the ever-present electrical energy and ceaseless formative constructive and destructive power, the universal propelling vital force, at once the propeller as well as the resultant. "The principle of unity builds the sparks (atoms) and places them in the six directions of space in wheels."

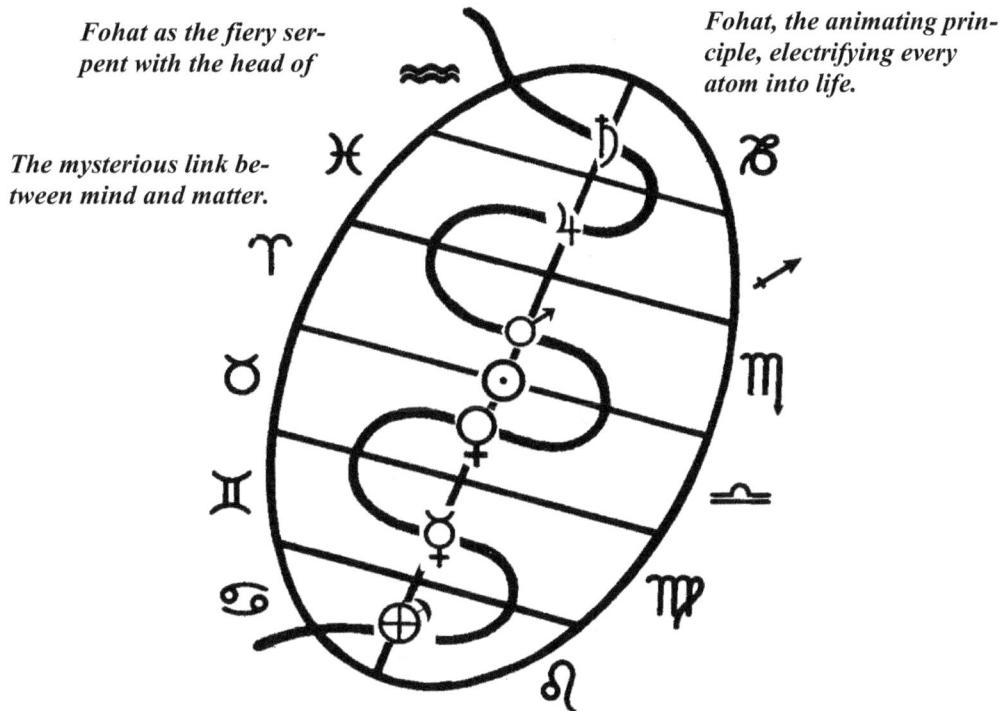

Fohat as the fiery serpent with the head of

Fohat, the animating principle, electrifying every atom into life.

The mysterious link between mind and matter.

The planets, placed in six directions (or divisions) of space, are neutral points. Therefore, it can readily be seen that a planet can have no individual sex, but is a perfect blend of both male and female attributes. Each planet functions through a male and female sign, but is itself bisexual.

The above illustration is the solar system pattern, the World Egg (or germ); it is also called the Mundane Egg, the Cosmic Egg, and Cosmic Atom, spun out of two substances made in one, Spirit-Matter, Father-Mother, Wisdom-Love. Our solar system is but one egg or cosmic atom in a universe teeming with millions of such eggs, all following the same perfect pattern. Of Fohat it is said "he is their guiding spirit and leader (of the atoms), he separates the sparks of the lower kingdom (the etheric) that float and thrill with joy in their radiant dwellings and form the germs of wheels. He places them in the six directions of space and one in the middle, the central wheel."

All the heavenly bodies have a dual force, and are bisexual in nature. This does not exclude the spiritual Sun, who is not only Father but Father-Mother to His creation. The Father side is wisdom, light, and life called Spirit, active and male. The Mother side is love, substance, and form, called matter, passive and female. When manifestation begins, the Mother side becomes active from within, fructified by spirit. Matter is a forever changing and evolving form, always pushed ahead by the spirit principle within it. Wisdom and love, the two Father and Mother principles working together as one. Form is crystallized love, never crystallized spirit, for spirit cannot be crystallized; love gives it body. It is the same in all workings of nature: both male and female are needed to create forms. Love is the female, formative principle that gives form to life. Male Spirit gives life to form.

We come to realize that there are no miracles. Everything in the manifested Universe, as well as the unmanifested Universe, comes about as a result of natural law. That which we might consider as magic is but the application of a higher law. To impress this upon our minds we will leave the realm of ancient teachings and consider the teachings of a seer.

Sri Yogananda, in his book Autobiography of a Yoga, says, ". . . all nature is governed by law. The principles that operate in the outer universe, discoverable by science, are called natural laws. But there are subtler laws that rule the hidden, spiritual planes, and the inner realm of consciousness." This confirms that we do not live in a universe that "just happened." It did not come about by accident. We are all a part of a Divine Plan, and everyone has a vital part to play. We are all important. We are cells in the body of God; one cell out of harmony inhibits the total function.

For an inner comprehension, quite different from intellectual understanding, we will again quote from the Stanzas of Dyzan as found in *The Secret Doctrine*. Again, I urge that you do not strive for objective understanding at the very first but let their inner meaning permeate your consciousness and sink deeply into your inner mind.

> The Eternal Parent (Space), wrapped in her ever-invisible robes, had slumbered once again for seven Eternities. Time was not, for it lay asleep in the infinite bosom of duration.
>
> Darkness Alone filled the Boundless All.
>
> Alone, the One Form of existence stretched boundless, infinite, causeless in dreamless sleep, and life pulsated unconscious in universal Space. There was neither silence nor sound; naught save ceaseless, eternal Breath, which knows itself not.
>
> The hour had not yet struck; the Ray had not yet flashed into the Germ; the Mother-Lotus had not yet expanded. Her heart had not yet opened for the one

Ray to enter, thence to fall, as three into four, into the lap of Illusion.

The seven sons [the planets] were not yet born from the Web of Light. Darkness alone was Father-Mother, Primordial Matter; and that was in darkness. These two are the Germ, and the Germ is One. The universe was still concealed in the Divine Thought and Divine Bosom.

The last vibration of the seventh Eternity thrills through Infinitude. The Mother [Space] swells, expanding from within-without like the bud of the Lotus. The vibration sweeps along, touching with its swift wing the whole universe, and the Germ that dwelleth in darkness, the darkness that breathes over the slumbering Waters of Life.

Darkness radiates Light, and the Light drops one solitary Ray into the Mother-deep. The Ray shoots through the virgin Egg, the Ray causes the eternal Egg to thrill and drop the non-eternal Germ, which condenses into the world-Egg.

Then the three fell into the four [cosmic, spiritual elemental]. The Radiant Essence becomes seven inside, seven outside. [Seven principles expressing through six planets and the Sun.] Although the Sun is not a planet, it is one of the Elohim [Sephirath], the creative principles.

The luminous egg, which in itself is three, curdles and spread in milk white curds throughout the depths of Mother, the Root that grows in the ocean of Life.

Darkness vanished and was no more; it disappeared in its own essence, the body of Fire and Water, or Father and Mother.

Behold, oh Pupil, the radiant child of the two, the unparalleled effulgent glory, Bright Space, son of Dark Space, which emerges from the great dark waters. It is the New Life [Universe], the Wisdom; the One is Four [elements], the four takes to itself Three [secondary Suns], and union produces the Seven [principles], in whom are the seven which become the Hosts and the Multitudes. Behold him lifting the veil and unfurling it from East to West. He shuts out the above, and leaves the below to be seen as the Great Illusion.

Father-Mother spin a Web, whose upper end is fastened to Spirit, the Light of the one Darkness—and the lower one is its shadowy end, matter; and this Web is the Universe spun out of the two substances made in one, which is Spirit-Matter. Then Father-Mother sent Intelligent Force to harden the atoms. Each is a part of the Web reflecting the Self-Existent Lord like a mirror, each becomes in turn a world. He builds them in a likeness of older wheels, placing them on the imperishable centers.

These quotations are but a fraction of beautiful Stanzas of Dzyan as found in *The Secret Doctrine*.

This is the abstract formula of cosmic evolution. The same abstract formula applies on all planes, to man, earth, solar system, uni verses, and on into infinity. There is no end; there can be no beginning. The constant appearance, disappearance, and reappearance of galaxies, solar systems, races of humanity, and individual man goes on ceaselessly; a regular tidal wave of flux, and reflux, all reappearing on the same eternal foundations, their own individual spiritual essence. The disappearance and reappearance of individuals we know as reincarnation.

Many of the advanced thinkers of our time accept this theory as being the only logical concept. On a grander scale it is repeated in the heavens as all the heavenly bodies live out their life cycle, fade back to their Source, and then again appear, in what Mr. Hoyle calls the expanding universe and science calls the conservation of energy.

Summary
1. The potential of all forms exists unmanifested in the Spiritual Sun, which is but another name for the Source of all life, God. This is not Jehova the Spirit of the Earth, but the Supreme Ruler of the entire universe.

2. He was also called the Formless Infinite. Being formless, He could not be seen but His Invisible Rays of Light are Life.

3. The Ten Sephiroth are abstract principles from which planets developed as density increased as they traveled farther out from Source. From them in time came centers of power, male and female, divided in order to manifest, each according to its own nature.

4. Duality, or sex, existed from the start, from the first out-breathing of activity from the Spiritual Sun.

5. Male spirit gives life to forms; female soul gives form to life.

6. Working together, manifestation begins, and the sun, visible symbol of the Invisible Sun, comes into being.

7. The organism of the universe is filled with planets; in esoteric terms the planets are organs in the body of God, the universe.

CHAPTER 4

MAN: THE ULTIMATE CREATION

Back in the far dim ages of antiquity, according to ancient occult teachings, when man first moved upon this Earth, he was a different type of being from what he is today. He was bisexual, etheric in form, and spiritual within. To our eyes today he would be invisible. He was, however, very much an individual, and much closer to the Source of all creation. He walked with God and he talked with God; not with a language of the tongue but by inspiration and inner understanding.

As the ages of time rolled on, the etheric form became denser and by natural evolution the being became two, male and female. This is where our Bible begins its history of man. The "days of creation" are understood to mean a period of time, not a twenty-four hour day. In Hindu occult literature they are spoken of as a Day of Brahma, and understood to mean many, many thousands of years of creation, the outbreathing of Creative Energy. The Night of Brahma, or inbreathing of Creative Energy, whereby all creation is drawn back to the Source, is the same length of time for rest and repose. They are comparable to our day of work and night of rest. The seventh day of rest will come after the six Days of Brahma, or when total creation is completed and the inbreathing of the Creator draws all back to the Source for a long period of rest before once again sending forth life forms to commence their journey, this time on a higher spiral of evolution.

It is important to remember that the biblical allegory of Adam and Eve is exactly that: an allegory. It is a symbolic narrative of the period when man and nature changed from an etherical form into a truly material and physical condition, a condition that was to prevail for many millions of years. Adam was a race of men, not an individual. They were called the Adamic or the Lemurian race. They were the fifth sub-race of the third root race of this, the fourth Round. A study of the Rounds and the races is a most fascinating and absorbing study. It is well worth anyone's time and trouble but cannot be gone into here as it is only an interesting sidelight and not a part of cosmic astrology itself. Many books have been filled with information and misinformation on this subject. I suggest that those interested enough to pursue it farther obtain a copy of *The Secret Doctrine* by Helena Blavatsky, an accurate facsimile of the original edition of 1888. This should be used by those interested in getting exactly the meaning that Madame Blavatsky meant to convey. Later students with good intentions have changed some of her statements into what they thought she meant to say, unfortunately making many mistakes.

Occult literature tells us "the Spirit unfolds, the soul grows, the body evolves." As the bodies of the Adamic race evolved to complete materiality, the androgyne form gradually changed from its bisexual body over long periods of time, each being becoming predominately male or predominately female, although having the latent organs of both, as we still have today. This did not take place in one man, Adam, nor in the period of one deep sleep as spoken of in the second chapter of Genesis. During the long preceding period, slowly evolving humanity was moving step-by-step into a material and physical condition according to cosmic plan in the blissful unawareness of childhood. The deep sleep was not a slumber as we know it but was more of a mental inaction or inattention, as of adolescence, for it was the pre-adulthood of the human race; a passing from primitive, racial childhood, leaving behind its innocence and its ignorance. Nature had been preparing and perfecting the human body in the minutest detail for the function of procreation. Organs of reproduction formed, the young were conceived and brought forth as they are now. The beings were no longer of a composite sex, they were human beings now, fully visible and material with a fully crystalized bony structure, completely of the flesh, or as stated in Genesis 3:21, "coats of skin, and clothed them."

Now death came upon the human race. Spirit cannot die, so former races had passed from one stage to another, changing but not dying. Even now death is but a change from one kind of life into another. The physical body becomes weary and worn out. It is discarded like a shabby coat that has outlived its usefulness. It returns to the material elements from which it was formed to be absorbed, until it once again is created into a human form, for we are all eternal beings in human form.

As the physical body of man evolved and man left the security of the astral world, Eden, we are told that man fell. In reality the fall is into materiality and not into sin. We are not paying for the "sin" of our ancestors, Adam and Eve. The "fall" or descent into material form is a very necessary part of our experiences, necessary for our soul's growth. The monad does progress and develop by progressively sinking, or if you choose, falling deeper and deeper into matter, thereby becoming in due time man, but always with the Spark of Divinity hidden within him. This descent into the density of matter, this 'fall' of man was into a material body of flesh with everything that goes with it including suffering and death. For although the Divine Spark cannot die, the envelope it inhabits does die, over and over again, thus developing in the monad a self-conscious immortality.

With fully developed man came the struggle for existence against the elements and the wild beasts. Eventually the very fight for existence caused man to descend into savagery. Dimmer and dimmer became the memory of his Divine heritage, but it never faded completely from his consciousness. In every cell of our being memory resides, and always, though dimly, our innermost conviction is of our Divine heritage. We never lose it but it has become dormant through long disuse.

Through the countless ages of involution, devolution, and evolution the forms of this life-wave have been going on, gathering experiences of life, learning from mistakes, passing through turbulent times of grief and joy, but continuing always its upward climb. Many times it seems that there is no use to continue; we fall and rise and fall again. Sometimes we are just too tired to go on. Overcome by the seeming futility of it all, we ask, "Where does it all lead? Who really cares after all?" But something within us will let us rest for only so long and then gives us a push onward on the upward spiral. We seem unable to quit for long. In the long ages of time, that which appears to us to be many years or even an entire lifetime is but a second in eternity. The lessons continue, the soul grows.

Our study of cosmic astrology shows us that everything must eventually return to pure Spirit, God. Everything goes through the same stages of development, from spiritual through astral, etheric and into material form, where we are now, and will continue to be for eons of time, except as individuals forge ahead of the masses on the evolutionary path. As degrees of density increase and the object, whether man or planet, becomes visible to material eyes, it loses its identity with its Maker. Now it must go forth to fulfill its destiny. In the beginning, God says in brief words exactly what all ancient scriptures teach: that before form of any kind existed, all existed in the Great Spiritual Source. The word "beginning" must be understood to mean the beginning of manifestation. There could be no beginning of spiritual force, for that which begins must also end, and spiritual force has no end. There are periods of inactivity or rest, but never an ending.

It is utterly amazing to me that so many of our advanced scientists, mystics and religious teachers without knowing the slightest thing about astrology—and caring less—are constantly making statements to verify ancient and Cosmic astrology without knowing that they have done so. Fred Hoyle in his excellent work, *The Nature of the Universe*, speaks of the appearance and disappearance of galaxies, solar systems, and all heavenly bodies. He also states that they go on forever. This can seem to be a contradiction unless correctly understood. They disappear and then reappear, recreated from the same elements, or as he puts it, "from the same background material." Occult teachings tell us that we reappear, recreated on the same Eternal Foundations. These spiritual elements can never be destroyed. In *The Secret Doctrine* we find: "The eternity of the universe as a boundless plane, periodically the playground of numberless universes incessantly manifesting and disappearing called the manifesting stars; the appearing and disappearing of worlds like a regular tidal ebb of flux and reflux."

This is from Swedenborg: "The visible kingdom is only a theater representative of the Lord's kingdom and this latter is a theater representative of the Lord Himself. There is but one single Source of Life, which is that of the Lord, and this Life flows in and causes man to live; to this life correspond forms which are substances, and which by continual influx are so vivified that they appear to themselves to live by and from themselves. This correspondence is that of 'the recipient organs with the life received.' The universal heaven is so formed as to correspond to the Lord, His Divine-human principle; and man is so formed as to correspond to heaven in regard to all and singular things appertaining to Him, and by heaven to the Lord. The heavens constitute as it were one man, which is therefore called the Grand Man between which and all constituted parts of every individual man, there is an exact correspondence."

People of all lands have as a basis for their sacred teachings a Spiritual Source, differing only in name. The Hebrews called their Supreme Being Einsoph, the Limitless Light. The American Indians had their Great Spirit, held in the same reverence and worship. Parabrahm of the Hindu, Brahma of India is also in every way the same as our All-Father, God.

At the start of manifestation when Force or Energy "moved upon the face of the deep" we have the beginning of the world as we know it today. Just the beginning, and many billions of years ago.

Everything manifested comes from, and ultimately returns to that Spiritual Sun of which our solar sun is a visible symbol. There are billions of solar suns, in billions of solar systems, in billions upon billions of galaxies out in interstellar space. We need be concerned with but one solar sun, our own light-by-day sun; only one solar system, our sun and its family of planets; only one galaxy, our own Milky Way. What lies beyond we will leave for others to determine. Our own system and the influence of its planets is a vast enough subject to occupy our time at present.

Space, or the invisible universe, fills the boundless all. It is of the material universe, forming as it were a protective shell around and encompassing the energy field of the Invisible Sun. Space is eternal, not in a sense of endless time but for the lifetime of the universe, unchanged and unchanging. It is self-existent, not dependant upon any other thing for its existence. It is a female principle containing the potential of all forms although forms had not as yet emerged. It is relative to "place," having a definite place in the visible universe but not reaching into the realm of the Invisible Sun. Since space does have limits to its boundaries it cannot be thought of as a limitless void as we sometimes hear it defined. It is neither limitless nor is it a void. Even in periods of inactivity it teems with life. It is called Prakriti by the Hindus, Chaos by the Greeks, the Eternal Parentless, that which is, was, and ever will be, whether there is a universe or not. However, the quality of that activity does change in the intervals of time between periods of manifestation. It is also referred to as "the Waters," not meaning liquid water as we know it but a fluid substance encompassing and interpenetrating all planes. Space is the body and container of the universe with its seven principles. Chaos is abstract space before the dawn of manifestation, the Egg containing all that was to be made manifest in time. The ancient sages called space the Eternal Mother because they said she contained within herself all potential manifestation, a living organism, never a mechanism. *The Secret Doctrine* says "chaos, the Great Deep over which Spirit is silently hovering in the first hour of reawakening."

Although space is dual in nature she is predominately female, emanating from the Mother side of Deity. Spirit, coming from the Father side of Deity is also dual but predominately male. Space is coexistent with Spirit; it holds the essence of substance as Spirit holds the essence of life.

Spirit contains the female attribute of soul. Spirit and space are two expressions of one activity, each with its own work to do. Although spirit is both male and female, to function it has to follow the laws of matter and divide into male and female principles. Therefore, the female principle soul was ejected forth to begin its work of evolving forms into manifestation. This is the soul of the universe, corresponding to individual soul. In all works or expressions of nature both the male and the female principles have to function.

Soul is the builder of forms, spirit the life within these forms. Spirit never becomes matter but fructifies matter with life. Individualized spirit is the ego of man, that part of us which never leaves the throne of God yet is forever with us. It is our link with God, the Divine part of every human being. Life within the universe is the same as the life within us. All life is spirit.

A function of space is to record pictures of all events, thoughts, feelings and emotions, both Cosmic and individual of man and beast. These are forever preserved in space and are called the Akashic Records.

Astrology deals with three energy fields, the energy field of the Spiritual Sun, of the solar sun and of the earth. The constellations also have an energy field, as does every object, manifested or unmanifested. In man it is called the human aura and may be seen as colors surrounding the individual by those who are sensitive enough to perceive it. The constellated energy field is described as "a gigantic energy field in interstellar space revolving around an unknown center." Its perimeter is called the constellated zodiac and is described as an imaginary broad belt in the heavens containing twelve constellations. The signs of the zodiac are named for the constellations and the influence they exert. We will not concern ourselves with the constellations or the constellated energy field, for its influence is upon the Ages of time and does not directly affect us and our daily affairs. An energy field consists of vibrations emanating out from a central source.

The energy field that surrounds the Spiritual Sun is described in the Kabala as being "like a fog." It was comprised of Love and Wisdom as One. It is invisible but contains all life, the divine life of the universe. This activity of the energy field of the Celestial Plane is expressed in *The Secret Doctrine* as: "When the One (the Spiritual Sun) becomes two (separate into Love and Wisdom) the threefold (union) appears, and the three are One."

Seemingly the first thing after manifesting His aura or Spiritual Energy Field with the Four Cosmic Forces or Spiritual Elements was to make the first law of physics, duality or polarity, male and female, by dividing His Potency into a Father- Mother God, Wisdom being God the Father and Love being God the Mother. From these two principle attributes of Himself and the union, all creation proceeded.

The second energy field with which we are concerned is the energy field of the solar sun. This contains the zodiac and the zodiacal signs, which are similar in their nature to the constellations for which they are named. The Earth passes through the influence of one of these signs every month beginning with the sign of Aries at the vernal equinox on about March 21 of every year.

The third energy field is that of the Earth. These twelve divisions are called the mundane houses and pertain to Earth alone. In the astrological chart they rule departments of life and indicate the department which will see the most activity throughout the life of the individual according to the planets which are found within it. Each corresponds to a sign and the nature of that sign, just as the sign corresponds to the constellation and the influence it exerts.

Fred Hoyle in *The Nature of the Universe* speaks of the energy field (or magnetic field) of the galaxies, the planets, the Earth and the Sun. It is a book on astronomy that is well worth reading. Among other things it brings home to one the immensity of space, the unbelievable vastness of the universe around us. It also points out the need for a joining of forces of scientific minds and spiritual teachings. One scientist to whom we owe a debt of gratitude for his work along these lines is Dr. Gustaf Stromberg. He was born in Sweden in 1882, and achieved world fame for his work in astronomy both here and abroad. He has written many books that show a wonderful comprehension of things spiritual as well as scientific. In his *Time, Space and Eternity*, written shortly before he died in 1962, he says, "it seems that the Eternity Domain is our real home, and from there we make short excursions to the physical world of space and time. During such a trip or trips we learn many lessons which may be helpful in our future development."

The sun, being as it is in the center of our solar system, is the giver of life for this system. It transmits the life-giving rays of the Father all out through our universe bringing life to all. It is the ego principle, not ego consciousness but the spiritual ego principle. Ancient scriptures define the ego as being "a pure spark of Divine Essence resting serenely on the bosom of the Infinite, calmly receiving and recording the multitudinous experiences of the soul." It is the spark of the divine in every living person.

Summary

1. The origin of man is God. But the origin of man on earth is his descent into matter, matter being but a condensation of the finer, spiritual substance into denser physical substance.

2. That humanity was first an ethereal being is a strange concept to many, and yet humanity of today still possesses an ethereal body. We are three-fold structures possessing the physical, the astral, and the ethereal bodies. The history of mankind thus repeats itself in every life.

3. The "fall" of man into the material body begins our journey through the rounds of evolution and finally, back to Source.

4. The spirit center of every cell of our being remains constant, a memory of past glory and a reminder of future attainment.

5. It is the soul, encompassing mind, that returns time after time to gain new experiences, more wisdom, deeper spirituality.

6. You can and do "take it with you," every bit of the real Truth ingrained in your consciousness remains with you forever.

7. Energy fields are vast magnetic fields that surround the heavenly bodies, but every object has its own energy field that can be detected by sensitive instruments.

CHAPTER 5

THE SECONDARY SUNS

We have spoken briefly of the three secondary suns in the chapter on spiritual astrology. We must keep in mind that these are not like the worker planets. They do not function as do the other planets in the solar system. They have a function all their own, vitally important and completely different. These are the Mother planets, the vessels of influx into which the Divine Light of God flows; the worker planets carry it into action with the help of the sun, which is the seventh principle into which the six are synthesized. They are also called systemic suns, for each functions through a working system of two planets and four signs. They rule planes of life, planes of action, not the action itself. Each holds its own radiant essence, sending it out into space to be picked up and used by the worker planets.

The three planes of action are the biological, the mental, and the electrical planes, represented by the planets Pluto, Neptune, and Uranus. Their influence flows forth as vibratory rays which blends and interpenetrates the fields of all the others. For instance, the mind realm of Neptune interpenetrates everything; everything is dependent upon mind for its very existence. The plane of Uranus, living electricity, the life essence of matter, also interpenetrates all planes, for it is that. which vivifies all things and gives them life. The life plane of Pluto certainly penetrates all planes. The most inert and seemingly lifeless clod teems with life. Each of these three secondary suns has its own particular work to do and carries it to completion with the help of its own worker planets and their system of signs. A complete study will be made of this farther along in this chapter and in the chapter devoted to the planets. Keep in mind these two facts: the planet is the principle; the signs are its functions.

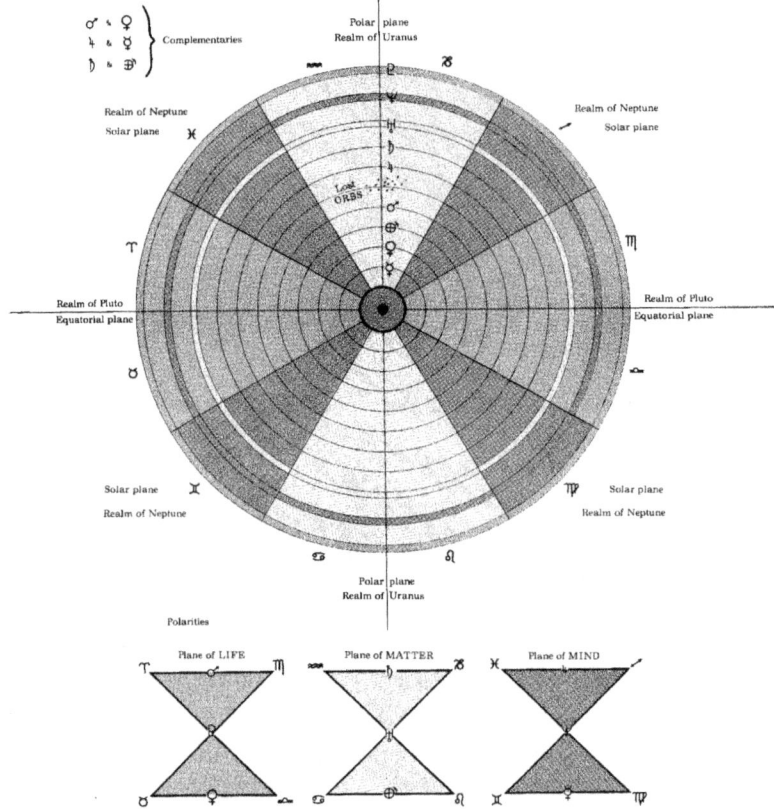

The three systems (or planes) and their rulers.
Polarities and Complementaries.

Study the shaded chart and note that Uranus, the first of the secondary suns which we are about to consider, revolves on a polar plane. That is, it has the greatest orb of influence in the polar region. Pluto revolves on an equatorial plane, Neptune on a solar plane. You will see that those planets which are under the rulership of each secondary sun have their signs in the regions specified. There is a great deal more that will have to be said along these lines later. These four solar bodies—the sun and the three secondary suns—are the organs upon whose action the creation and evolution of our planet earth depends.

To be able to really understand the shaded illustration it will be necessary to have an understanding of the symbols used. Without this knowledge it would be impossible to get a true picture of the nature of the planet. Symbols are not merely an abbreviation, a short and convenient way to designate meaning. On the contrary, it is a pictograph designed to tell a story or impart some information. It could be called an esoteric shorthand. It was known to the initiates of old and employed as a reminder of the hidden meanings that were being taught to the student. Now for a study of the symbols themselves: O is the symbol of spirit before manifestation began, life with no beginning and no end. Put a dot in the center and it depicts the beginning of manifestation, ☉ and ☽ is that arc which O ejected from itself, the female principle, or soul, or mind.

Is there a correspondence here between this symbol and the "Adam's rib" from which the Bible says that woman was formed? Any place that this symbol is used, or simply ☽, signifies the mind or soul principle. In charts, ☉ is the Sun, ☽ is the Moon. The + symbolizes the cross of matter. These symbols are used in various ways and combinations for the planets and the signs. Venus is shown with this ♀ as its symbol; reading the correct meaning we have spirit descending into matter. Mercury, ☿, is spirit descending into matter guided and watched over by mind. Mars, ♂, is spirit aiming higher, upward, or force expended in a heavenward direction—the motor principle of spirit. Jupiter, ♃, is the principle of mind over matter. Saturn, ♄, is the principle of matter over mind, for Saturn deals with the materialized world in which we live. Nevertheless, mind is very much there—deep and serious thought is a part of Saturn's nature. The symbol for earth is matter enclosed in spirit, ⊕.

The symbology for the secondary suns do not follow the same exact pattern as they are of recent rediscovery and have been named by the astrologers who discovered them.

Uranus was found by an amateur astronomer named Herschel in 1781. It was called Herschel for a time but later came to be called Uranus as it had been in ancient times. The H seems to stand for Herschel, the complete symbol being ♅. Neptune was rediscovered in 1846 by Johann Galle. The symbol for Neptune is ♆. Pluto was not located until 1930, by Clyde Tombaugh. The symbol for Pluto being is ♇, and it seems to be merely the P and L of Pluto.

Of the ten heavenly bodies in our solar system which have an influence upon Earth and its people, there are six active worker principles which are synthesized in the seventh, the "central wheel," the sun. These seven are the creative principles of nature. There are also three latent (not visible or apparent, and therefore, hidden) principles which are the secondary suns. The sun, giver of life within our solar system, contains the potential of all manifested life; the secondary suns draw from it that particular vibration peculiar to its own needs, each acting as a repository for the life-giving elements that have been held for redistribution as needed.

The ancients did not call these solar bodies planets; they called them "gods" and wove myths and legends around them to better illustrate their nature and universal influence. A myth is different from a fantasy inasmuch as a fantasy is entirely a product of someone's imagination that is related for the purpose of entertainment. A myth is an account of a great truth told in symbols, often in a humorous and colorful manner, but designed to impress upon the mind of the listener the information it contained and which they wished to have remembered.

Uranus, ruler of the electrical plane, works through Saturn, the principle of crystallization, and our own Earth, as the arena of action, together with Earth's helper, the moon. Mythology tells us that Uranus ruled the heavens and the ethers until he was dethroned by his son Saturn. The Stanzas tell us how "Father-Mother sent intelligent force (Saturn) to harden the atoms" from etherical substance into material substance. Everything had been of an etheric nature until the crystallization principle hardened the atoms. Everything that came into being after Saturn took over was of a dense material form. For long ages Earth had been in an etherical condition—a body of gases, scientists would say. Its people were described as ethereal without and spiritual within. This was the condition that existed at the first half of the third race of this fourth Round in which we are now living, the Adamic or Lemurian race. Over a period of many millions of years the etheric form of man became fully clothed in flesh over a bony frame. They took on a "coat of skin" as told in Genesis 3:21. (We are now the fifth Race, the fourth being the Atlantean. There are seven sub-races to each Root Race, but that is a study by itself.)

Mythology has kept for us many of these ancient truths, but like all else mythology has passed through many hands. It has been added to, parts not understood have been removed, and in many ways has not retained the original meanings. Mythology tells us that Saturn dethroned his father Uranus as the ruler of the universe. The very word "dethroned" may bring to mind the picture of a mighty battle in which might overcomes right and a rightful ruler dethroned by rebellious subjects. Such was not the case, of course. Instead of being overthrown as ruler of the etheric universe we will think of Uranus as delegating some of his duties to his son Saturn through the process of natural growth and evolution. Colorful and picturesque word-pictures were employed to impress upon the minds of the people these stories and their symbolic meanings. There were no books in those days to record these teachings and so other means had to be used to preserve the lessons.

When Saturn by Divine command had hardened etheric atoms into material ones, Earth became much as it is today. However, although Saturn dethroned his father as the ruler of the material universe, Uranus is still very much the ruler of the etheric world. Since Earth has become so material, Uranus now rules from within. He, as living electricity, is the vital life and motion of matter. We live in an electrical universe; everything is of living electricity, the very life essence of matter. Without Uranus, all the universe would be static, lifeless and dead.

The two worker planets of Uranus are Saturn, Earth, and the Moon are shown on the next page.

Saturn functions through time and cyclic progress by means of backward (Capricorn) and forward (Aquarius) motion on all planes. He is sometimes called Father Time, and often pictured as an old man with a scythe over his shoulder or in his hand. Form began when Saturn took over, and also time. Old illustrations showed Saturn holding an hourglass as well as the scythe.

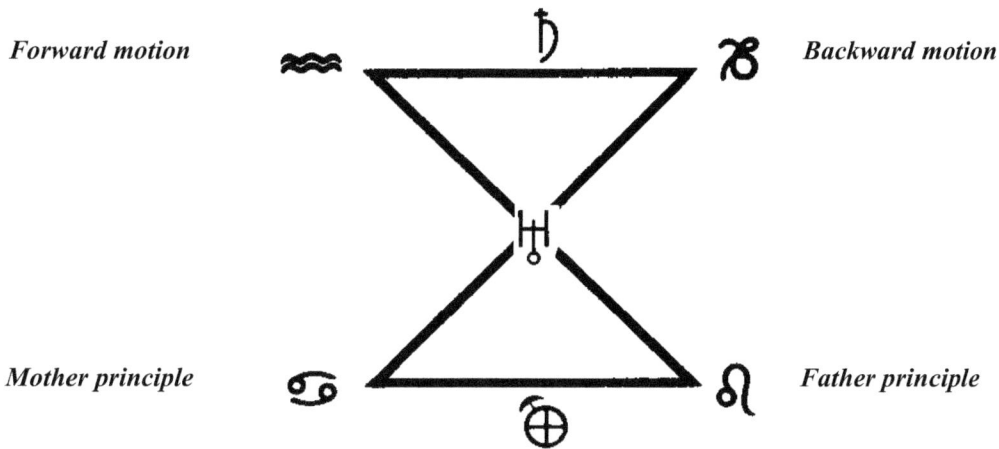

Forward motion ♒   ♄   ♑ Backward motion

⛢ ☿

Mother principle ♋   ⊕   ♌ Father principle

Earth and the Moon, as coworkers, rule all Earth's people, men and women, high and low, fathers and mothers. We wish to emphasize that although we—and all astrologers—use the term "the Sun" as a term of convenience, it is never the Sun, always the Earth, that passes from sign to sign. The Kabala says that "the spirit of the earth is as [much a creator in his own realm as is the spirit of the heavens, they are twins, interchangeable in function when not acting as two in one." For the most part the poor Earth is ignored and overlooked by the astrologers, but how can it be? It is here; it has to be considered. It is the principle of strength through strife. Just how it affects the rest of the solar system we cannot know, but we can feel sure that in a universe where all is used for mutual help, one planet of the ten will not be thrust aside as of no consequence.

Examine the shaded illustration (page 36) now and see how the plane of Uranus is at the top and the bottom of the circle; in other words, in the polar planes. Blue is the color of Uranus, like our atmosphere, which appears blue from outer space. The orbit of Uranus is shown as the light-tint circle; the light-tint sectors show the signs through which the two worker planets function in Uranus' realm.

Mythology deals with the ruler of the biological plane, Pluto, in the following fashion: The gods had cast lots to see which duties would be assigned to each in regard to the just-created Earth. Uranus had inherited control of the electric, vivifying principle of life itself. To Pluto fell the task of caring for the life and death of form, of all life on earth. He would have to stay within the Earth and never be seen on the outside. This was fine for awhile, but one day he got to thinking of all that was probably happening on the outside; he wondered how the various gods were progressing, how Jupiter, for instance, was getting along making laws within nature for Earth and all its peoples to follow. He decided to just step outside for a brief moment and see for himself what progress had been made now that summer was over and harvest was at hand. He wanted to see just how the laws were working. He stepped outside his domain just as Cupid, Venus' mischievous little son had decided to try out a little law of his own that he had just thought up. The law that he had decided to try was that whoever he shot with his bow and arrow would fall in love with the first person or thing that his eyes fell upon after being shot. As unknowing Pluto stepped forth from his domain, his eyes fell upon Persephone, the seed, ripe for harvest; at that moment Cupid let fly an arrow which found its mark in Pluto. True to the just-enacted law, Pluto promptly fell in love with Persephone, gathered her up in his arms, and disappeared with her into his underground kingdom where he made her his wife and queen.

Persephone's mother, Demeter, the goddess of growing vegetation, became very worried and went to Jupiter; she told him what had happened. "Now that Persephone, the law of the seed, is underground with Pluto," she asked "what is to become of the vegetation upon the new and barren earth?" Jupiter agreed to have an understanding with Pluto, which he did, resulting in a very definite law that when vegetation went to seed, Persephone would go home to her mate in their underground kingdom for a certain period of time, for the purpose of germination and gestation. She would then go back above ground to her mother, the goddess of growing vegetation, to give birth to her offspring, which Demeter, her mother, would do her best to care for tenderly. But then when the harvest was at hand again, and the vegetation gone to seed she would return home to the underground region.

This is a perfect example of the truths that are hidden and yet revealed in old mythology. The story of the "rape" of Persephone is simply a tale of natural law, at work in nature itself, repeated year after year. There is no such thing as rape in nature; everything is according to law. Persephone, the seed, did not need force but sank willingly and happily into the warm open arms of the great law, content to let the mortal part of her die that the soul within her might live again in la new day of manifestation. In *The Secret Doctrine* we read that "nature is feminine and passive, and the spirit principle which fructifies her is concealed." Pluto is the concealed, fructifying principle within the earth and soil. Pluto, together with Virgo, rules the seed.

Everything in the heavens has its counterpart in man. Pluto's rule extends to anything that has to do with life in form, so in the human form the region under the supervision of Pluto is the abdomino-pelvic cavity below the diaphragm, the underworld of our physical bodies, not the underworld of crime and gangsters. Neither Pluto nor any other heavenly body rules over this part of our manmade underworld! Only man with his "evil imagination" could rule over the conditions found there. Pluto is the fructifying principle and rules the biological universe of life in form, the life center in everything.

In the shaded chart (page 36) Pluto's orbit is outlined as a medium-tint circle, his realm on the equatorial plane are the medium-tint sectors. Here are the four signs ruled by Pluto's two worker planets, Mars and Venus:

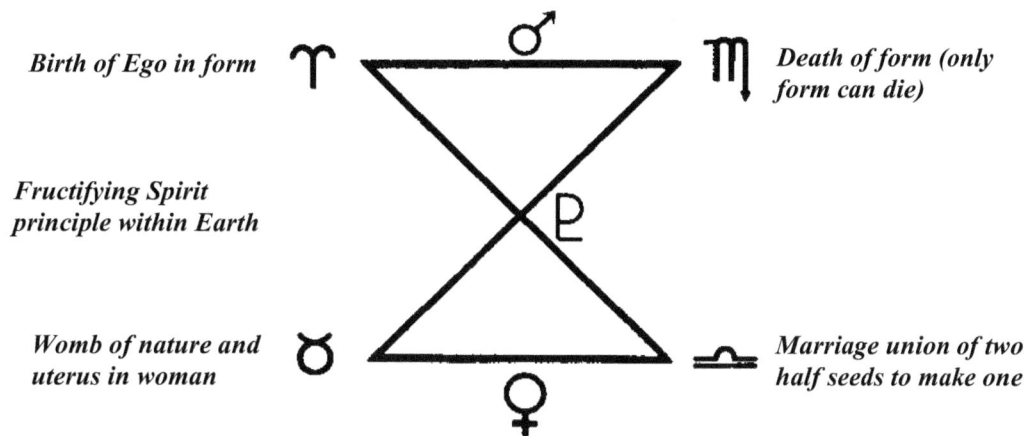

Birth of Ego in form ♈ ♂ ♏ Death of form (only form can die)

Fructifying Spirit principle within Earth ♇

Womb of nature and uterus in woman ♉ ♎ Marriage union of two half seeds to make one

♀

Venus is the mating principle, the first law of nature. It brings together the two half-seeds of the male and female to make one. Mars takes the joined half-seeds and builds a body to house the incoming Ego. Mars is the builder, sustainer, and final destroyer of form. The ancients never thought of Mars as a god of war except in protection of the body he had built. He is the principle of force, energy, and construction; also of destruction when the old has outlived its usefulness and must be destroyed to make way for new construction. The study of embryology is an absorbing study; through it one can observe the various planets at work, cooperating with each other, each doing a perfect job in its own realm. There will be a great deal more along these lines in the following chapter.

The third of the secondary suns, Neptune, revolves on a so-called solar plane as its vibrations seem to include the whole solar system. Neptune rules the whole mental plane, and mind certainly penetrates all. There is no place in all the universe where mind is not actively present. The rays penetrate like sunshine. The realm of Neptune is represented by the heavy-tint sectors and its orbit is shown as the heavy-tint circle. In these heavy-tint sectors you will see the two worker planets, Mercury and Jupiter, under the secondary sun, Neptune, and their four signs occupy the solar plane of Neptune.

According to mythology, Neptune was given rulership over the surrounding waters. This is not the waters on the Earth; rather, Earth's moon has charge of these, governing tides and all waters on the earth. The surrounding waters refer to the mental and astral realms, the Divine Mind of the universe. Jupiter and Mercury are the two mental planets, Jupiter being the subjective mind, the inner mind of nature, Mercury is the objective mind and the five senses.

Neptune rules the psychic realm in the universe and in man. It rules all mental action. It is the "psychic wireless," the contact point between human mind and universal mind. It originates and holds the Divine blueprint or mental plan which is then carried out by Jupiter or Mercury. If individuals are not advanced enough spiritually or mentally to respond correctly to a prominent Neptune in the chart, they may bog down in their own mysticism; or the analytical, factual mind of Mercury gets in the way with resulting confusion. After the principle of crystallization was established and forms became material, the principle of law, Jupiter, took over. Mythology says Jupiter dethroned his father, Saturn, and now rules the universe as the principle or natural law. He is to rule until Typhon, the principle of disintegration, begins his work and the Inbreathing of the Creator draws all back to the Source. The mental realm of Neptune is illustrated thus:

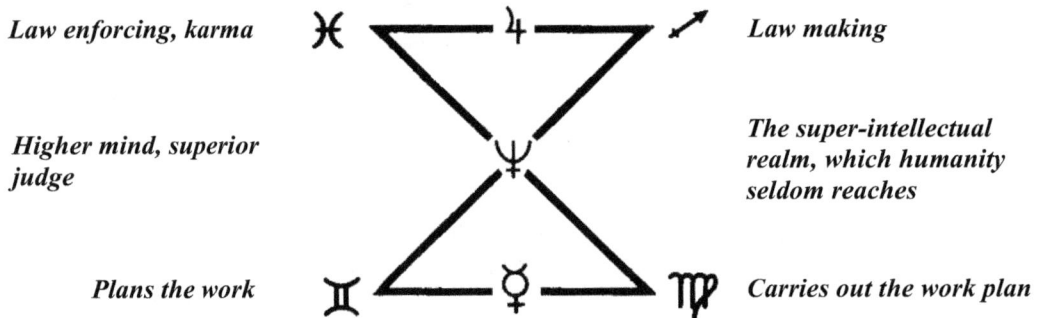

Law enforcing, karma ♓ ——— ♃ ——— ↗ *Law making*

Higher mind, superior judge — ♆ — *The super-intellectual realm, which humanity seldom reaches*

Plans the work ♊ ——— ☿ ——— ♍ *Carries out the work plan*

Jupiter is the principle of law, all laws. Mercury is the messenger of the gods (laws) on all planes.

When we synthesize the illustrations of the three secondary suns we have a complete picture of the solar system as shown on page 43. These three secondary, systemic suns were well known to the ancients, who did not place them in their charts because their influence is universal rather than individual. Their use in a chart is somewhat overrated; however, they do have an influence, and when correctly understood they do add interest to a chart.

Each of the two planets belonging to the realm of a secondary sun functions in a somewhat different manner. Both are on the same plane, but one works on an inner or subjective plane while the other works on an outer or objective plane. These are known as the coworkers, each supplying a vital property to complement and complete the work of the other.

In the realm of Uranus, Saturn works on an outer plane, crystalizing the bony structure of the body so that it may stand upright. It could be said that it also supplies a "mental backbone" because of the deep and serious thought that is a part of Saturn's nature. Earth, with the help of the Moon, works on an inner plane, covering the skeleton with a coat of skin, forming the vehicle for the etheric as well as the astral and physical bodies.

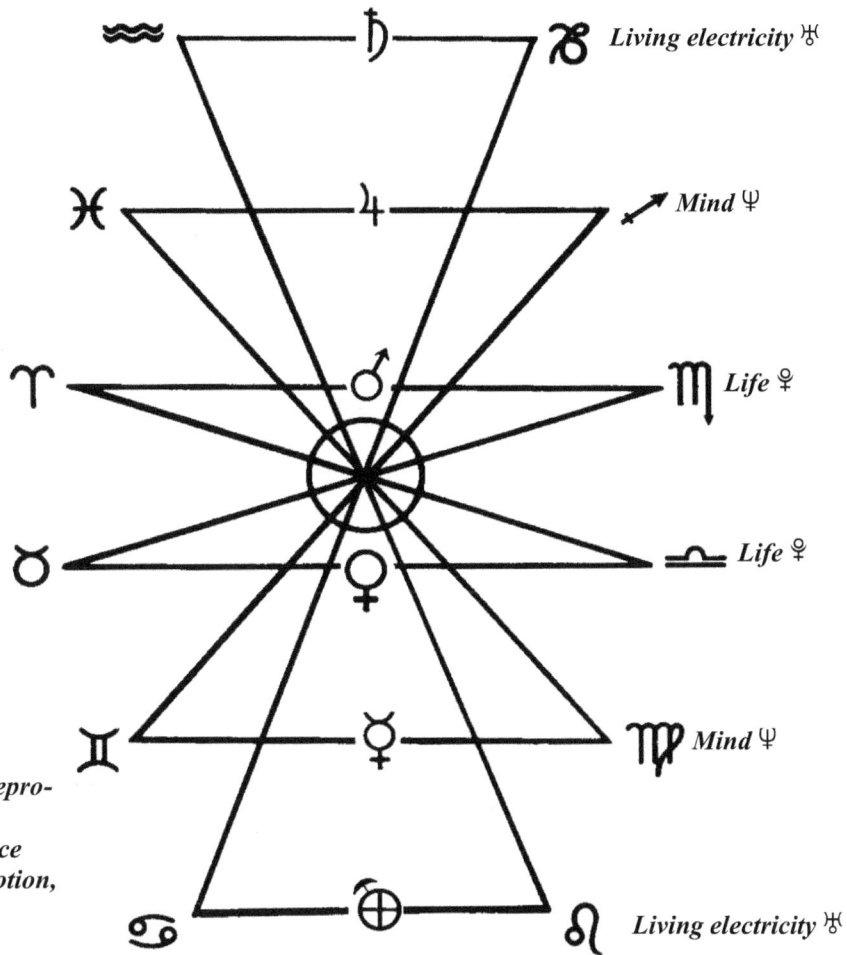

≈≈   ♄ ──── ♑ *Living electricity* ♅

♓ ──── ♃ ──── ↗ *Mind* ♆

♈   ♂   ♍ *Life* ♀

♉   ♀   ♎ *Life* ♀

♊   ☿   ♍ *Mind* ♆

♇ *biology, life repro-*
duction
♆ *mind substance*
♅ *electricity, motion,*
action

♋   ⊕   ♌ *Living electricity* ♅

In the realm of Pluto, Venus works on an inner plane, in the subjective realm of beauty and love. In the protective inner warmth of the mother's body the new body is conceived as the two half-seeds are brought together. Mars, on an outer plane, sees to the task of building the body for the incoming personality.

In the realm of Neptune, Jupiter works on an inner plane. It is the inner mind of nature, the subconscious mind in man, not the spiritual mind, for that has to be developed by our own efforts. Mercury works on an outer plane, the objective, reasoning, analyzing mind. The five senses are used for the impressions received for the analyzing and weighing process.

Summary

1. The story of the secondary suns is to be found in ancient manuscripts. Their concepts are perpetuated in old mythology.

2. The ancients knew of the existence of these three. They knew they ruled planes of life and that the influence they exert was primarily over cycles of time, with a relatively minor influence on individual lives.

3. Symbols tell a story. They must be recognized in the fullness of their meaning wherever seen.

4. As the colorful word-pictures employed by the teachers to impress upon the minds of the students the ancient truths of creation lived through the ages, they became myths.

5. Pluto guards the outer perimeter of the solar system, keeping the planetary vibrations from being lost in interstellar space. It is the farthest from the sun in distance, but distance (like time) has no reality in the abstract realm, so the abstract influence is the closest to the sun. The sun is the giver of life; Pluto is life, the ruler of the life planes.

6. Uranus is very much a part of the material universe, which is crystalized atoms, but the life of the atoms is electricity, the living electricity of Uranus.

7. Humanity as a whole is approaching a time when the high frequency rays of Neptune will be used as an aid to psychic and intellectual advancement. Only a few of our more advanced leaders are able to respond adequately at the present time.

8. Each secondary sun expresses on an inner and an outer plane; each of these planes is represented by a planet. This pair of planets is called a coworker or complementary as each is needed by the other to complement and complete their work.

9. The colors of the three secondary suns correspond to the three primary colors. Red is an active color and belongs to Pluto. The force and energy of Mars and the mating function of Venus respond to red. The blue of Uranus is seen in our own atmosphere as viewed from outer space. The mental realm of Neptune, which penetrates all like sunshine, is yellow, the color of Wisdom.

CHAPTER 6

THE NATURE OF THE PLANETS

It is necessary to keep firmly in mind just what a planet is: a concrete heavenly body of solid or semi-solid substance embodying a Cosmic, Divine principle, and sending forth radiations of that principle into space. We must also know that it is not the light from a planet that carries the influence, but the vibrations. Light is of the material universe and it takes many years traveling through space to reach us from even the closest neighboring planet. Vibrations are of spiritual substance, and as such are unhampered by space, reaching us in a steady, unchanging radiation, constantly pouring out their influence upon us, and upon everything in the solar system.

We will use the planet Mercury to illustrate what we mean when we speak of a concrete object with an abstract principle. Mercury is a material planet; we see it often in the morning or evening sky. But this material, concrete object radiates forth the abstract principle of intelligence. All mental pursuits, scientific studies, and learning relative to the objective mind comes under the rulership of Mercury. We receive help in our studies and aid in ferreting out facts and analyzing our findings when Mercury is in a favorable position or sign. We meet obstacles, frustrations, and delays when it is in a position or sign that is not favorable to the nature of Mercury. It is the same with each planet. Each is a material object receiving from the sun, through one of the secondary suns, that radiation peculiar to its nature which it passes on into space through one of the twelve zodiacal signs.

These radiations are modified by the nature of the sign the planet occupies at that particular time. If it is one of the signs governed by the planet, the planet is then said to be "at home" or in its home sign. It has a stronger and truer influence than when in a sign ruled by another planet.

Each planet also has a sign of exaltation where it has a potent strength. This exaltation is not the greatest power of the planet, but it is the completion, or the finishing expression. It is a special function, the apex, the point of manifestation. The law of the triangle is action, reaction and interaction. The exaltation of a planet corresponds to the interaction, the product.

If a planet is in the sign opposite to its exaltation, it is said to be in its "fall." When there, it has no force of expression and thus is not a great influence in the natal chart. When the planet occupies the sign opposite to its home sign, it is in its "detriment." When found there it is hampered in the true expression of its nature, for the nature of the sign is opposite to the nature of the planet. The home signs express the true nature of the planet; the detriment modifies the nature of the planet according to the nature of the sign. We will give more time to a study of the home signs, detriment, exaltation, and fall in the chapters on the planet and signs.

On page 47 is a drawing of a natural chart with the point of Aries at the eastern horizon. This will change in the individual natal chart according to the time of day the individual was born, but the house is still influenced by and retains the nature of the sign in the natural chart. Remember that the signs are divisions of the energy field of the sun. The sun is in the center and therefore in all signs equally and at all times. The other planets journey around the sun in their own orbits, cutting through the line of vibrations of each sign in turn. It takes the Earth about thirty days to go from sign to sign, the Moon only about two and a half days. The other planets vary according to their own rate of speed and their distance from the sun.

The mundane houses are divisions of the energy field of the Earth and are designated by number. They rule departments of life and show each person where he or she will encounter experiences that will contribute to advancement and the soul's growth.

As we return to a study of the nature of the planets, it again becomes evident that it seems to be our fate to differ with most of the popular concepts of astrology. So many times when our present-day astrologers describe the nature of a planet they describe the way human beings respond to the influence of its vibrations. Since we are all in different stages of development, both mental and spiritual, we react in different ways. As illustrated in a former chapter, an evolved Mars personality would react to an injustice with typical Mars force and energy, but in a controlled manner. One who was not spiritually advanced would react with anger and vengeance. The force of Mars would be used in both cases, one in a constructive way, the other in a total waste of energy. The nature of Mars is used in the one case and misused in the other. It is no fault of Mars, however, that its force is misapplied. It is entirely an improper human reaction.

Planets are organs in the body of God (manifested nature); they are attributes of God. Can anything evil come from God? There are no evil planets, no evil signs, no evil houses, or evil aspects. Our lives are what we make of them, how we respond to the vibratory force from on high.

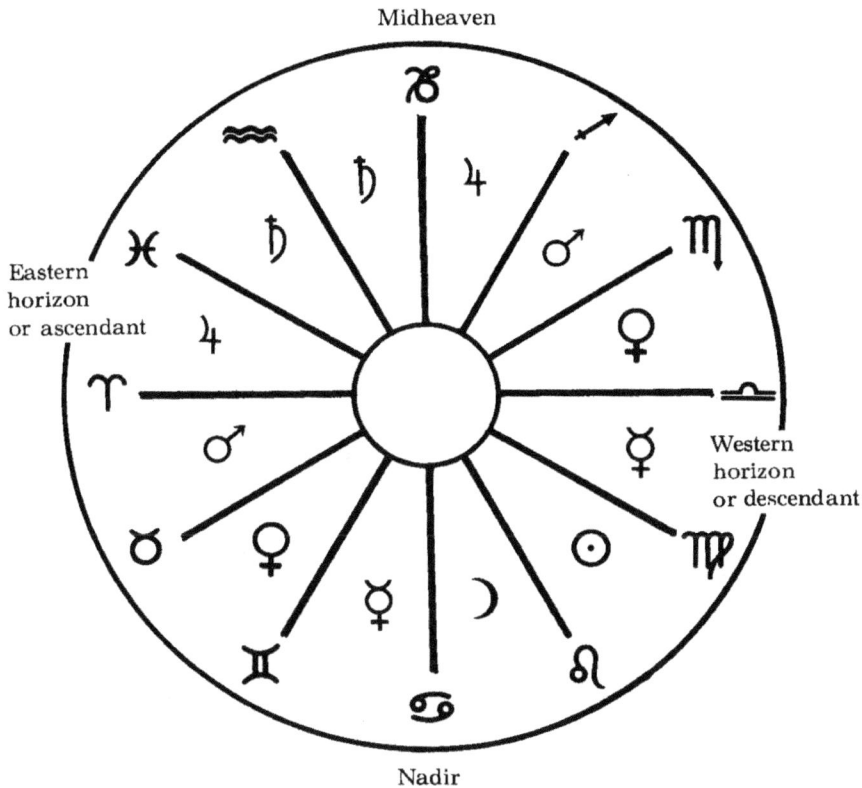

Natural Chart with signs, houses, and ruling planets.

The concept of Mars and Saturn as the Lesser and the Greater Malefics is unworthy of consideration. Evil is an invention of mankind, it lies within his own being, of his own making. It is never imposed upon him from without. Genesis says, "man's imagination was evil from his youth."

All the planets are bisexual; each contains both the male and the female attributes and the Father and the Mother principles of Deity. Active male and passive female attributes have separated on the abstract plane, but flowing together, working together, interpenetrating all planes, express as definitely male or definitely female on the material plane as the functions of these planets and the zodiacal signs. All nature must make use of both the male and the female in order to create. So must each planet function through a male and a female sign. It could be no other way, for the planets could no more break the laws of nature with impunity than could lesser bodies.

It is common practice to call the signs positive and negative instead of male and female, but the word "negative" has come to be regarded as something weak and undesirable, a bad influence, so it gives an untrue picture of the qualities to be found in the female signs. In reality the positive is outward-going, active, seeking, forceful, and male. The negative is passive, accepting, retaining, nourishing, and female. The positive is plus, the negative minus, but astrologically there is no plus or minus, just a difference. One is as completely necessary and indispensable in the grand scheme of creative nature as is the other. They are two different expressions of the same creative power. Henceforth, we will use the terms male and female, just as the ancients did, because they are more in keeping with the true nature of the signs and thus more useful and descriptive than the terms "positive" and "negative."

These two opposite expressions of the same creative power are known as polarity, which Webster defines in this way: "that quality or condition in virtue of which a body exhibits opposite or contrasting properties or powers in opposite or contrasted parts or directions." The Church of Light defines it thus: "It is an established fact, a law of physics that every action is accompanied by an opposite and equal reaction. Therefore, for every positive force in the universe there must be an equal negative force. If it were otherwise, the energy expended in one direction would not be accounted for in another and might become lost."

The planets are bodies which expend forces by means of the zodiacal signs which they are said to rule, and through which they function. The sign is a cosmic function, a medium of expression for the planet. They work through all the laws of nature, including physics.

Keeping in mind that planets are attributes of God and thus are organs of expression of Divine Principles, we will now go on to a study of the nature of each. We are dealing with principles of life, the material representative of which are the planets.

We will take a portion of the illustration on page 20 to enlarge upon to clarify the concepts that we will put forth in the following pages.

From the electrical plane of Uranus come the planets Saturn and Earth with Earth's helper, the Moon.

The Sun corresponds to the heart in the human body. It is the cosmic heart, the central power house of the entire solar system. It is due to that power that all within the solar system proceeds in an orderly fashion. It is the cosmic proton, the center of the cosmic atom (solar system) around which the cosmic electrons (planets) revolve. Since ancient scripture tells us that "the sun and the earth are twins, interchangeable in their function when not acting as one," we will consider them together first, then individually.

Earth is the arena of action, the principle of strength through strife. There is a theory that every solar system has its Earth—the planet of trial and error, of learning through doing and making mistakes, which is certainly the only way we do learn. Earth is said to be the most difficult planet to live on, and that its hardship gives the soul the greatest opportunity for development. So the ancient term for Earth, that of the arena of action, promoting strength through strife, has added significance. We have no way to know just how its influence is felt on other planets, but we do know that the science of the heavens is an exact science so it would be difficult to believe that any one of the ten planets would be of no use to the others. Each of them has a definite work to do; each of them has an influence that is felt by the others and is a help to them in their allotted destiny. The Sun and the Moon rule the vital forces and supply to our bodies the life forces of nature. The Moon rules the vital force in men, the Sun their constitution. In women the Sun rules their vital force, their vitality, and the Moon their constitution.

The spirit of the Earth is as much a creator in its own realm as is the spirit of the heavens; Earth is a creator of forms with the help of the sun. Without the sun, Earth would be a barren waste; nor could the sun alone support life without the help of Earth. All through astrology the term "the Sun is in the sign" is commonly used, so we will follow along the familiar way. You will know, however, that the sun is in the center of the solar system and in all signs equally and at all times. It is Earth that moves from sign to sign, occupying each for thirty days and moving on into the next.

The Sun's (Earth's) male sign is Leo, and its symbol, ♌, represents the male organ of reproduction in an upright position. The ancients called it "the organ in which God dwells" because it is the only organ capable of producing human life; to them it was holy, representing the Divine Creative Principle. It is the father principle. The female sign is Cancer. Its symbol, ♋, represents the arms of the mother cradling a babe to her breast, the Everlasting Arms guarding and nourishing the young. This is the mother principle. Earth's helper, the Moon, is directly in charge of Cancer. Moon rules gestation (the pre-natal period), birth, mothers with their protective tenderness, nourishment, humility, and the guiding, guarding, growth and development of the child. It influences all home and domestic life, and rules women and the love life of men. It is the soul principle, the formative principle of the astral form.

The Sun rules men, and the love life of women. It also rules the ruling classes, pride, self-esteem, hope, firmness, consciousness, spiritual love (as different from the mating love of Venus), all truly inspired creations of art, and the fine arts. The animal chosen to represent the sun as a living symbol was Leo the lion, a regal, royal animal, king of the forest and jungle. We illustrate the unit of Sun-Earth and the Moon thus:

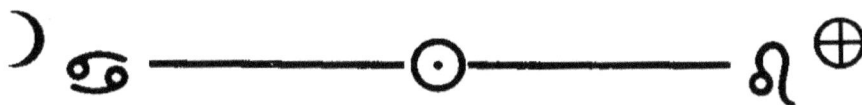

Modern astrologers say that the Crab is the living symbol for Cancer, but in the days when astrology was understood in its true form the crab was never the symbol of Cancer. This is a later addition, someone's idea of an improvement. There seems to be no record of when this change came about. The ancients knew the Cat to be the living symbol for Cancer, the domestic replica of the jungle king, gentle, affectionate, the most perfect mother in the animal kingdom. Just when or why the crab was substituted for the cat as the living symbol for Cancer no one seems to know. Certainly there is not the slightest likeness between the crab and the holy principles of motherhood embodied in the zodiacal sign of Cancer.

The home signs of Sun-Earth and the Moon are Leo and Cancer. Their opposite signs of Aquarius and Capricorn are the detriments. The exaltation of Sun-Earth is Aries. This is the point where the sun crosses the equator on the return to the northern hemisphere, bringing life and growth to a barren world. The exaltation of the Moon is Taurus. Taurus is the cosmic womb, the uterus in women; the Moon rules gestation and the growth and development of the babe in the womb. Taurus is also the storehouse of cosmic substance, corresponding to the nourishing principle of the Moon. In ancient times the cow was the living symbol of Taurus instead of the bull as is used today. Just why the bull was substituted remains as much a mystery as the substitution of the crab instead of the cat for Cancer. It is a bit ridiculous to consider a female bull! The opposite signs of these exaltations are Libra (opposite Aries) and Scorpio (opposite Taurus). These are the planet's fall, no strength of expression. Wrong response to the influence of the Moon can bring about laziness, restlessness, a lack of responsibility. They are adaptable people, but must beware of inconstancy.

The negative human reactions to the influence of the Sun can result in self-importance, arrogance, tyranny, a domineering nature, and boastfulness. In other words, an excess of the good principles wrongly directed and applied can lead to difficulties.

For the present we only wish to establish the relationship between the planets as principles, and the signs through which they function. More about the signs will follow in the next chapter.

Saturn, the other planet of the plane of Uranus, is sometimes called the Great Malefic. Present-day astrologers have robbed Saturn of one of its functions. They have chopped off an arm and given it to Uranus, thereby robbing it of the function of the forward motion of Aquarius, leaving only the backward motion of Capricorn. What would happen to cosmic equilibrium if both backward and forward motion were not used? Certainly there could be no progress. One wonders if a planet robbed of one polarity would be able to remain in its proper orbit. Saturn has been deprived of the male quality, leaving only the female. Nothing can operate with half its powers removed; no planet can fulfill its destined work without both the male and the female functions. There can be no forward motion without backward motion. That which seems to be retarded motion is but the backward thrust that propels forward action; it is a necessary withdrawal to gather energy for the surge ahead. The exaltation of Saturn is Libra is the Balance. Certainly balance is necessary in the backward and forward action of progress. Evolution and progress depend upon Saturn. Far from being the Great Malefic, Saturn is the planet of restraint and protection. Saturn rules the tenth and eleventh houses through Capricorn and Aquarius, the houses of ambition, friends, and hopes. The mother is usually represented in the tenth house and the influence of Saturn can be likened to that of a mother protecting a wayward child from ill-considered activities and expenditures. Saturn puts the brakes on. We have to earn all we get from Saturn. Never does it bestow with the free hand of Jupiter, but it does not withhold from us through malice, only from a restraining influence for our own protection. If punishment is measured out it is but to instruct.

Saturn's functions are illustrated thus:

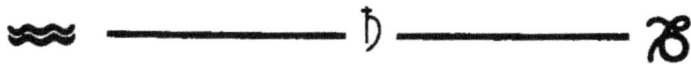

$$ \approx \quad \text{———} \quad ♄ \quad \text{———} \quad ♑ $$

The principle called Saturn is the principle of crystallization. We read that at the beginning of manifestation "Father-Mother sent intelligent force (Saturn) to harden the atoms. Each is a part of the Web [Universe]. Reflecting the Self-Existent Lord (Sun) like a mirror, each becomes in turn a world." As the crystallization process of Saturn started, Fohat gathered the crystalized atoms of fiery dust and formed them into planets. In man, as the etheric form was developed enough to become more substantial and visible, Saturn hardened the atoms into material ones, forming the skeleton, and the material body of man became the vehicle for spirit and soul. Spirit can never be crystalized, so man remains one part spirit, one part astral or soul, and one part physical. These constitute the human trinity. Thus we have the bony structure of our bodies, all the joints, teeth, inner eardrum, even the hair, all ruled by Saturn. Saturn rules self-control, order, stability, hard work, depth of mind and balanced thinking.

Some so-called authorities have assigned to Saturn the purely human reactions of avarice, self-ishness, timidity, fear, and a tendency to become morbid. A moment's reflection will show that these are but an excess of the true nature of Saturn. Deep and serious thought can become fear and anxiety; protection of possessions can become avarice, selfishness, and a morbid fear of want. If Saturn is afflicted in the birth chart, it but maps the tendencies we must learn to control, rising above them to the higher expression of Saturn. Before we leave Saturn and its many duties, there is another thing we must mention. Saturn brings us to old age through all kinds of experiences, and when death is near, this old Father Time with his scythe gathers all our life experiences and lessons and closes them up within the seed to be brought forth in the next generation.

Now we will consider the planets of Pluto, the life plane, which are Venus and Mars. First we will consider Venus, for it is Venus who brings together, through Libra, in the womb of Taurus, the two half-seeds to start the growth of a new physical body. Venus is the mating principle, the first law of nature. Libra rules the union, the act of procreation (Leo rules the male organ), without which there could be no creation, and the uterus, within which the seed is deposited. As we pointed out before, Venus rules human love and the mating instinct; the more spiritual aspect of love is ruled by the Sun. The two arms of Venus are illustrated thus:

$$\text{♉} \text{————————} \text{♀} \text{————————} \text{♎}$$

Venus rules the love principle within nature; the Sun rules the love principle in the universe. Venus also rules social affairs, love of fun and mirth, affection, friendship, appreciation of beauty, sound, color, and form. Venus rules the arts, but not the fine arts. The truly inspired creation of art is ruled by the Sun.

The human excess of Venus qualities can lead to perversion, lust, laziness, sensuality, deprivation, and an inclination to shallowness. The exaltation of Venus is Pisces and the explanation for this will follow as we show how Venus and Mars cooperate in their functions.

The principle of Mars takes over after conception has taken place. Mars is the builder everywhere, in the cosmos and in the body. The Ancients called Mars "the builder of the Palaces," and it has the help of all the Elohim, the builders, or worker planets. Mars takes the substance provided by earth—the food, prepared by Mercury (through the process of digestion and food chemistry)—and builds a physical form for the new embryo. Saturn is hard at work hardening the atoms for the bony structure. All this proceeds according to law (Jupiter) and order (Saturn). There is not one of the working principles that is not represented here. Moon rules gestation and the birth of the child. Besides the food as building blocks that Mercury provides, he is also the breath of life that the newborn baby draws into the lungs in order to live. Jupiter is very much present as the subconscious mind that accompanies the new entity, as well as the workings of natural law.

Mars rules the head through Aries, but also the sewerage system of the body through Scorpio. Here again the complete cooperation of the coworker Venus is necessary. Mars through Scorpio eliminates the solid waste from the body through the colon and the rectum; Venus eliminates the liquid waste through the kidneys and the pores of the skin. Venus rules the filtering system of the body. Together they work to keep our bodies cleansed and renewed. The two arms of Mars are illustrated thus:

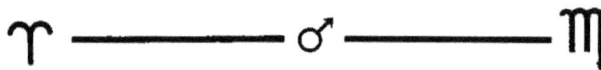

$$\text{♈} \text{————————} \text{♂} \text{————————} \text{♏}$$

Mars rules the cells of the body, not only the building of new cells but also the destroying of old and worn out ones. Scorpio carries the dead cells away as waste in order to make way for the new ones. Mars has long been called the god of war and so he is, but never the destructive wars of mankind. If this were a true concept we would have to accept the theory that war is a sacred principle, divinely created and divinely decreed. Mars fights to protect the body he has built. He defends it against an invasion of germs and infections. All the force and energy of Mars is directed against invaders of the body, the protector from within, who, with his army of cells, produces fever and heat, and conducts a war of defense against infection.

He disintegrates the dead cells and builds new blood corpuscles in the marrow of the bones. He is the leader, the motor principle of spirit, the energy force of ego consciousness, through Aries as I AM. With this concept of Mars to consider, is it likely that Mars is ever a sex planet? Scorpio has its own function to perform. It rules the colon and rectum. Would it be consistent with the laws of nature that this be a fitting abode for the beginning of a new, pure life? No! Venus has under her rulership the reproductive act of union under Libra, and the uterus under Taurus, in which the new life is safely housed, protected from any impurities. These are the organs nature provided for the sacred union and creation of new life. The region of Scorpio could not house a developing embryo. It is Venus that houses the embryo safely enclosed in "the surrounding waters," the amniotic sac of Pisces, exaltation of Venus. It is protected from shocks and injuries to complete its growth with Mars busily at work building and constructing the body to house the incoming ego.

The exaltation of Mars is Capricorn, the coordinator. All the principles cooperate in order to create, and the function of Capricorn is the coordination of all principles within the form. Capricorn's function is cooperation and coordination. Growth proceeds under Mars in the God-directed internal workshop that is in every plant and tree as well as animal life and in every human cell.

Every human cell contains forty-six chromosomes or genes—except the sex cells, the sperm and ovum, which contain twenty-three each. Consequently they could not produce by themselves. They must join in order to produce a complete cell or seed. These genes contain the hereditary particles that influence the transmission of parental characteristics from parent to child. They are brought together by Venus through Libra, via the phallus, under Leo, in the womb, under Taurus. By the law of attraction the waiting female ovum chooses one sperm from among the thousands, draws that one to herself, and the two become one flesh. This is conception; all other sperm respectfully withdraw. The ego enters at the moment of conception and always through the sperm, which may be either male or female, while the ovum is always female. Thus it is the male sperm that determines the sex of the child. Now it is a completed seed and the function of Pisces under Jupiter comes into being. We know that Pisces rules prisons; the embryo is protectively imprisoned in the amniotic sac for nine months while a marvelous process is going on inside by the six creative planets, the workers. When the six have finished their work, the amniotic sac opens and the little prisoner is released. Now Mercury has another function, that of breathing into the nostrils the breath of life, and the little entity becomes an independent living being. Mars continues the building of the body all through life.

Wrong human response to the influence of Mars could result in violence, excess, anger hatred, jealousy, vengeance, arrogance and a lack of consideration for others, instead of the energy, constructiveness, initiative and force that is the true nature of Mars. Mars is the builder, manager, sustainer, cleanser and defender of our bodies—a friend, not a malefic.

Neptune rules the mental realm, the surrounding waters. Again we must reiterate that this is not the waters of earth, the oceans, seas and rivers, but the waters of the ethers, the mental realm.

The two planets of the realm of Neptune are Jupiter and Mercury. They are both considered mental planets, ruling sciences, study and all mental pursuits. They have physical functions, too, of course, just as there are mental functions for the other worker planets. Every atom, every cell has an intelligence, a mind function of its own. All the principles cooperate in their functions. None works independently.

The supporting structure of the universe is law. Jupiter rules nature and natural law, mental and spiritual law, and even the habit law we forge for ourselves. If we break these laws—and we have free will to break them if we choose—we must expect to pay the price. This is the law of cause and effect, which is also known as the law of karma. It is not a punishment or reward dealt to us from high but a natural balancing reaction resulting from our own action. If we insist on thinking of it as punishment we must at least realize that we are punished by our sins not because of them. Jupiter rules law, the Will of the Creator expressed on all planes.

Jupiter rules the subconscious mind in man. This is the inner or instinctive mind. It is not the highest spiritual or superconscious mind; that we have to attain through our own efforts by rising to the highest expression of and combining the functions of Jupiter and Mercury. The subconscious mind is formed by what has gone before, impressions we have received from our earthly life experiences, often without benefit of Mercury's analytical reasoning. Jupiter rules religion, philosophy, benevolence, reverence, jovial good cheer, higher education, dreams, and intuition. It also rules prisons and hospitals for those who insist upon breaking the laws—civil, criminal, or the laws of health. The two functions of Jupiter are illustrated thus:

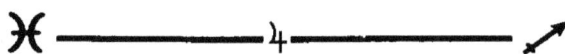

$$\text{H} \longrightarrow 4 \longrightarrow \nearrow$$

Male Sagittarius is the legal department that makes our laws. Pisces is law enforcement, the police department, judges, and the courts. It is the law put into operation. Modern astrology has left the making of the laws to Jupiter through Sagittarius, but has removed the power to enforce them by assigning Pisces to Neptune. Of what use is the making of laws if there would be no way to enforce them?

Jupiter is a big planet and does things in a big way. Often Jupiter bestows with a free and generous hand, but it is not all benevolence. Try breaking the law and see what happens! Saturn might warn the criminal with the idea of giving them another chance, but not Jupiter. "The mills of the gods grind slowly, but they grind exceedingly small" is a very apt description of the way Jupiter operates. Much time may go by and to all appearances the law-breaker is quite literally getting away with murder. But there comes a time when retribution must be made and Jupiter is quite merciless. Stay within the law (moral, civil, and criminal law) and Jupiter is the benefic that we like to picture. But break the law and watch the results. There is no avoiding the laws of nature. We cannot change this, nor can we rule the stars, but we can cooperate, stay within the law, and reap the benefit of Jupiter's benevolence. The exaltation of Jupiter is Cancer, ruled by the Moon, the soul principle. The final judgment is the judgment of the soul.

Jupiter is the principle of the law of mind over matter. It impresses the Divine pattern on mind substance in every living thing. Mind is the builder. As a man thinketh in his heart, so he is. Our inner mind, under Jupiter, shapes our actions, shapes our very bodies, and makes us what we are. Jupiter rules that inner urge that causes us to look inward and upward, and carries the conviction that although we have an animal body, we are soul, the highest expression (Cancer exaltation).

An excess of Jupiter's already expansive nature would be bombastic conceit, love of display, indolence, gambling, confidence games, and a tendency for shady transactions.

Mercury is the intelligent principle, the Cosmic brain functioning through the human brain and nerves. Mercury was known as "the messenger of the gods" in mythology. This illustrated the fact that Mercury served all the principles, all laws, through the telegraphic system of nerves carrying impulses and messages from all parts of the body to the brain. Place your hand against a hot stove and see how fast swift Mercury sends the message to remove it.

Mercury rules the outer expression of mind—the objective mind. The two arms of Mercury are illustrated thus:

$$\text{♊} \text{———} \text{☿} \text{———} \text{♍}$$

Gemini is the childlike mind—quick, restless, versatile, never satisfied. These people originate ideas, are clever, and try many things, often going from one idea to another with bewildering rapidity. Often they do not think things through to conclusion but leap ahead to the next interest. The Virgo mind is a more mature mind that excels at analysis; however, these people can delay action indefinitely in order to acquire more and more facts. A Gemini may write many books or articles, but is apt to write too soon and before all facts are assembled, while a Virgo waits too long, trying to do the impossible in a quest to acquire every bit of information pertaining to the subject. Virgo takes all details and analyzes them, pulls them apart and puts them together again.

Mercury rules respiration and the lungs, through Gemini. It has been said that a shallow breather is a shallow thinker, and it is certainly true that deep breathing, not only in the Gemini-ruled lungs but also in the Virgo region, the abdomen, results in deeper and more analytical thinking; but it must be deep breathing, in and out, up and down. Swift Mercury, as the messenger of the gods, rules expression and communication on all planes. On the physical plane, in the human body, the messages are sent via the nervous system, which Mercury also rules. He rules speech, thoughts, analysis, calculations and mathematics, studies, writing, language, and above all, expression. The sign of the Moon in the natal chart indicates the nature of the mind and how it works. The sign of Mercury shows how that mind expresses itself, the way it communicates. Advertising and publications are ruled by Mercury and the third house, as are short journeys of the mind such as childhood studies. Jupiter rules long journeys of the mind as well as travel. Long journeys into the realm of religious and philosophical research are a part of Jupiter's (ninth house) realm.

Mercury, through Virgo, rules the virgin seed before these two half-seeds are brought together in the womb of Taurus. As the two half-seeds are joined into a perfect seed pattern, there is also the inner memory and consciousness. A cell cannot think nor reason as it does not have that kind of intelligence; but it does have consciousness and memory.

The seed is an electro-chemical record of an infolded idea. All impressions of a sufficient strength to be impressed upon the inner mind are carried over into the instinctive mind of the new being; they are infolded into the seed, a part of the subconscious mind influencing the bodily structure, the beliefs, and characteristics of the individual. These are the genes, the characteristics inherited from both parents. Everything is born from a seed. Pluto rules the seed with Virgo. Mercury is known as "the conductor and reconductor of souls into and out of incarnation" via the fructified seed. Mercury has nothing at all to do with sex, nor has Mars. This is another function completely. Mercury is the keeper of the virgin seed, Mars builds the form after conception, Mercury breathes into the nostrils the breath of life at the birth of the child, and Mars continues to build, protect, and cleanse the body. Mercury is the food chemist who rules the alimentary process which begins in the mouth (under Gemini) and continues through the small intestine (under Virgo). Surely they are busy enough and have duties enough of their own to perform without man attempting to assign to them the duties of Venus. Mythology says that Mercury and Mars were brothers. It would seem so by the way they cooperate and work together in the body.

Wrong application of the Mercury intelligence could result in trickery, cunning, conniving, and dishonesty.

The exaltation of Mercury is Scorpio. This is contrary to what has been declared by some astrologers, but consider for a moment the function of Scorpio. In the physical body Scorpio carries away the debris so that the work of the builders may progress. In its own region, the colon, the food stays for several hours while the properties to be used for building blocks of the body are taken up by the blood for distribution to various parts of the body. Scorpio gets right to work eliminating the waste, sending it out of the body by way of the rectum. In the mental realm Scorpio is the fault-finder looking for imperfections. Gemini thinks and gets ideas, but leaves it to Virgo to carry them out. Virgo takes these ideas, some of which may not be so good, and analyzes them. After Virgo has completed the analysis, Scorpio takes over and really gives it the once-over. If there is anything wrong, Mercury in Scorpio will find it. When you see a chart with Mercury in Scorpio, the individual is capable of being a trouble-shooter; give this person a problem that has baffled others and the solution will be found. If the individual is spiritually advanced, he or she will be an invaluable addition to any organization; if not of a higher plane, however, the individual is apt to be disagreeable, critical, fault-finding, and not at all a pleasant person to have around.

This is a general analysis of the planets. I have purposely neglected to mention the asteroids, the lost orbs, for they have no place in astrology. They are of interest only in a general way. They have their orbit between Mars and Jupiter. No one knows how they came into being, nor what purpose they served. Some have speculated that they are the remnants of a planet that was pulled apart by the gravitational pull between Mars and Jupiter. It may be that a planet never fully developed. Or it may be that in the long ages before the seven workers took over, when Earth and the solar system were still in an etheric condition, this planet came into being. After Saturn dethroned his father, Uranus, the planet had no further function and began to disintegrate. It has been likened to baby teeth. They come into being, grow a short time, are no longer needed, and so disintegrate. Maybe at one time this planet had a function. No one knows and we may never know. It is not important in our study of astrology.

We have studied the principles embodied in the planets. Before closing this chapter we will consider briefly another point of interest that may help to fasten these concepts firmly in your mind.

Ancient astrology shows us the correspondences between things heavenly and things temporal. Everything in the heavens is there for a purpose; every planet in our solar system has its representative as a center in our human bodies. We are a copy—and a pretty exact copy—of the Supernal Man, the universe, the material body of God. The microcosm follows the prototype of the macrocosm.

These centers which exist within us respond to the vibrations from the planets in what is known as an urge. An urge has been defined as energy generated by a simple sensation of thought. It is a mental force exerted in a known direction. Usually we do not know why we are impelled to think or say or do a certain thing at a certain time. We may call it a hunch, a feeling that we should do it that way. If we cooperate, we usually find the going easy and productive. Sometimes we allow our objective mind to interfere; we reason away the impulse and find that we have lost an opportunity.

The Sun is the power urge, promoting pride, self-esteem, and firmness. The Moon is the domestic urge, ruling love of home and offspring. Mercury is the intellectual urge, increasing our desire for mental pursuits and knowledge. Venus is the social urge, encouraging friendship, fun, and togetherness. Mars is the aggressive urge, promoting energy and forging ahead in spite of obstacles. Jupiter is the religious urge, that tendency in man to look above the animal being for the real personality, the immortal part of man. Saturn is the safety urge, with order, restraint, self-control and secrecy.

The secondary suns are of such a universal nature that the same terms can hardly be used. However, Uranus, under whose rulership the Earth upon which we live, breathe and have our being, does have an influence that can be classified. It is called the individualistic urge. It promotes independence, originality, unconventionality, and inventiveness. Those people who are noticeably under the influence of Uranus, those with Uranus on the Ascendant or at the Midheaven, are individuals who are set apart. They like to function by themselves and not according to usual practices. They depart from established customs and pioneer in new fields or use new methods in old fields. They are restless people, an urge that must be channeled along useful lines or it will result in a total waste of energies.

Neptune has been tentatively identified as the Utopian urge, embodying high and majestic ideals. This would seem to be in connection with the description used formerly, that of the psychic wireless. In other words, it may be that Neptune attempts to bring out into objective consciousness our vague longings to be better people, to do noble acts for the betterment of all mankind, and perform all kinds of brave and wonderful deeds.

Pluto? Well it seems that much work remains to be done before we can accept an urge that adequately describes the nature of Pluto. The closest seems to the universal urge, denoting group activity for the benefit of all humanity.

As we advance morally and spiritually we learn to cooperate with these urges instead of opposing them. Then we find our lives becoming more harmonious, difficulties and frustrations having for a large part disappeared. This cannot be due to any change in the planets behavior. It is entirely due to the change in our response to the planetary vibrations.

I might say just a word here on the fascinating world of magic. We know that the universe is ruled by law. Jupiter allows no one to break its laws with impunity. However there are higher laws than those we customarily use, the higher expression of Jupiter's own laws. That which we consider magic is but the application of these higher laws. Einstein's unified field theory states that magnetism, electricity, and gravity are all manifestations of one force. By the proper use and control of any two, the third is nullified. Therefore, when electricity and magnetism are properly used and controlled, would it not be possible to nullify gravity? Where then is the "magic" of levitation?

All principles function on all planes. Each has its own realm where it reigns supreme, but it works tirelessly and unselfishly with its brother planets.

Summary
1. A planet is a physical object embodying an abstract principle, radiating its influence out into space by means of the signs through which it functions.

2. Every planet is an organ in the body of God through which divine principle manifests.

3. Each planet is functions bisexually through a male and a female sign.

4. All action in the entire universe is due to polarity, or sex, which is the foundation of all life, energy and consciousness.

5. We are a replica of the heavens. The vital centers in our bodies each correspond to a planet, and that principle cooperates smoothly and efficiently with every other principle. There is no struggle for supremacy, no attempt to do another's work.

6. Human actions can alter the true meanings of the influence of the planets, but as we evolve we rise to the higher expression of their principles.

7. To speak of an "evil" planet is to say that God has evil qualities since all heavenly bodies are attributes of God.

8. An urge is a mental or vibratory force to which we respond, usually unknowingly.

CHAPTER 7

THE NATURE OF THE SIGNS

When we open the ring of the zodiac we have the body of Supernal Man. Bringing it into our own region, closer to us, it becomes our own upright bodies, patterned after and an exact replica of the heavenly Man. Now a pattern emerges whereby we can see the smooth cooperation of the coworking planets and their pair of signs. Everything is duality and everything expresses through polarity.

The signs are divisions of the energy field of the Sun, and the zodiac is the boundary of this energy field. Signs have been described as sounding boards from which the vibrations of the planets are transmitted to us, each sounding board modifying the effect of the vibration according to its nature. The signs are of our solar system alone, and although they bear the same name as the constellations, they are not the constellations.

Constellations are groups of stars outside our solar system but still within our galaxy, the Milky Way. They are separated from our solar system by the vast distance of four light years. When we stop to consider how fast light travels, it dawns on us that a light year is a tremendous amount of time and distance. Our finite minds seem incapable of encompassing such figures. Visualize something like the diagram on page 62.

Eminent astrologers who should know better use the words "the planet was in the constellation Aries, or Libra, or Cancer." No planet ever leaves its orbit to be in any constellation! These astrologers do not distinguish between a sign and a constellation. The gravitational pull of the sun holds each planet in its orbit; it is in the sign, it stays within the energy field of the sun.

Symbol	Body Part
♈	Head
♉	Throat, Neck
♊	Shoulders, Lungs
☽-♋	Breast, Stomach
☉-♌	Heart, Spine
♍	Small Intestines
♎	Reproductive System
♏	Colon, Rectum
♐	Thighs
♑	Knees, All Joints
♒	Legs below knees, Ankles
♓	The whole Foot

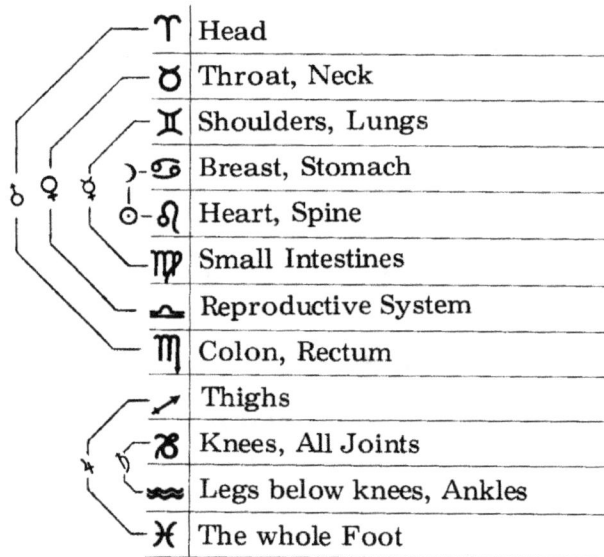

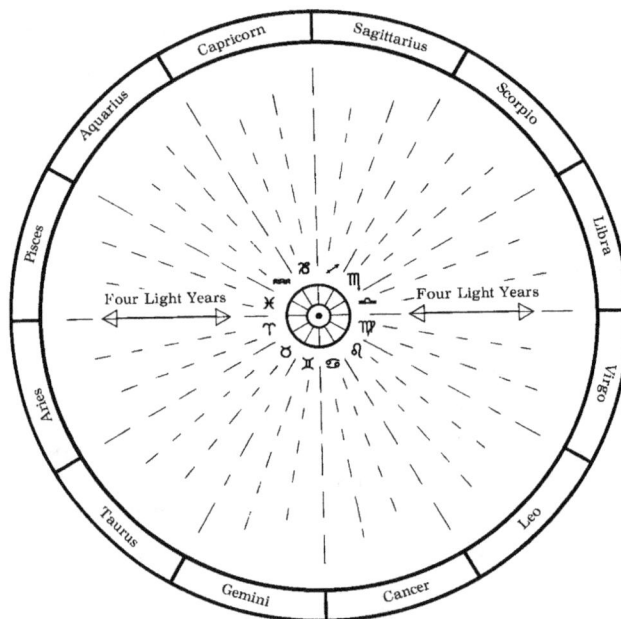

The solar system with the sun in the center and the signs within the energy field, held within the zodiacal perimeter. The outer ring is the constellated zodiac containing the twelve constellations that send the radiations of their influence into space.

Each of the twelve signs is named for one of the twelve constellations, which it resembles in nature. Just as the sign radiates a certain vibration that goes through the entire solar system, so does each constellation radiate vibrations equal in nature but immensely different in degree and scope of influence as they reach out into interstellar space. It would take the light from a constellation four light years to reach earth, but the vibrations being unhampered by time and distance, reach us immediately and their influence is constantly with us. Their influence, however, affects the cycles of time, the astrological Ages. For instance, the first point of Aries is now pointing at the constellation Aquarius, putting us in the Aquarian Age. For the past two thousand years it has been pointing at the constellation Pisces. We were then in the Piscean Age. This subject, that of the precession of the equinoxes, is a study in itself and can be found in any good book on astronomy.

We hope that we have fixed firmly in your minds the picture of each planet moving at its own rate of speed, in its own orbit, cutting through the lives of vibratory influence emanating out from the constellations and into the signs.

We will digress a bit here and comment briefly on a subject that is confusing to most of us, that of the apparent motion of the heavenly bodies. We see that phrase so many times that after awhile we find ourselves wondering if anything actually moves in the heavens after all. "The apparent path," the apparent movement, simply means the way it appears to us here on Earth. All heavenly bodies move throughout space, but not as they seem to us to move. We have such a restricted viewpoint from this little speck of dust called Earth. We know that Earth and other planets move around the sun, yet to us it appears that the sun moves around Earth, rising in the east each morning and progressing across to disappear in the west. This is the apparent path of the sun; yet the sun with its family of planets does have an orbit. The fact that it takes two and a half million years to complete its orbit removes it from the realm of our immediate interest.

There are four classifications for each sign, each of which must be thoroughly understood. First is to determine if the sign is male or a female, thus determining if its influence is active or passive. This is easy, the male being fire or air, the female being earth or water. The second consideration is to know to which element it belongs.

The third classification is that of quality. Each sign is either gaseous, solid, or liquid. Those that are gaseous are the starters, the movable and pioneer signs, which are also called the cardinal signs as they stand at the four points of the compass. The ones designated as being of a solid quality are the fixed signs, the finishers, the perfecters, those who stand solidly by what they believe. The signs of liquid quality are the developers, the mutable or common signs.

We might say that the movable quality expresses the nature of the element to which it belongs in its highest state of activity, the fixed quality expresses in the lowest state of activity, and the mutable quality is of a medium state of activity—the happy medium between the excessive activity of one and the unmoving resistance of the other.

Through a combination of these characteristics we will find ourselves with such strange combinations as solid water, gaseous earth, and liquid fire. Nevertheless, these are very apt descriptions and will tell you a great deal about the nature of that particular sign.

The fourth consideration is the degree of emanation. The first four signs, Aries through Cancer, are of a first degree emanation. They express true of their nature with perfect freedom of expression. The next group of four, Leo through Scorpio, is of a second degree emanation. These signs are modified in their expression by the workings of the mind. The expression of the third group, Sagittarius through Pisces, is modified by circumstances and environment. Each group has a keyword which describes its action. Freedom is the keyword for the first group, moderation for the second group of four, and the third group has the keyword of restraint.

Mars functions through the first sign of the zodiac, the sign on the eastern horizon, male Aries. Aries is a fire sign, gaseous in quality, and of a first degree emanation. Gaseous fire seems more potent and dangerous than ordinary fire so we come to the conclusion that an Arian person must be handled with extreme caution. All the force and energy of Mars is seen here, and the fiery enthusiasm and pioneering nature through inspiration, instantly from within, rather than modified by mind or by circumstances. It would be very difficult to stop burning gas. It would be equally hard to dampen the fiery enthusiasm of Aries. Neither one will be confined nor dictated to by another. It is easier to give way before them and let them have their own way. They are hard to hold down and will not be held back.

Aries rules the head of the physical body. He is the engineer, the manager of the whole system. With Mercury he rules the brain. He gives the orders for others to follow, a natural leader and starter of projects. This sign rules consciousness, the God consciousness made manifest. It is the ego consciousness, first manifestation of the universal consciousness of the Creator but individualized in every human being.

The keyword of Aries is I AM. Their best quality is leadership and their worst is officiousness. They can butt in like a Ram, but sometimes we also find an Aries person who must be more likened to a lamb, and it is interesting to note that the ancients sometimes used a lamb as the living symbol of Aries instead of the ram. Aries is the birth of form in the human body, the entry of the ego. "All that the Father is I AM, but I must attain it."

Venus functions through the second sign, female Taurus. It is of the earth element and solid in quality. Solid earth is very stable, and Taurean people are among the most stable in the world. They are practical, patient, quietly determined, and very fixed in their beliefs. Since they are of a first degree emanation, they express the solidity of earth without being influenced by anyone else or the circumstances they might find themselves in. They do not jump to conclusions, as do the gaseous quality folks. They will make sure they are right and then be completely unmoving, steady as a rock. They are the finishers, the perfecters; they will take what others have started and finish it. The Venus nature is easily seen here as they are good-natured workers, but they do not turn aside for any obstacles. Their very stubbornness makes one wonder if the term "bull-headed" did not come into use somewhere after the living symbol for Taurus was changed from the cow to the bull. A female bull indeed!

Taurus rules the Cosmic Womb and the uterus in women, as well as the neck, throat, voice box, all occult reproductive principles, and the "occult potency of sound." These people are often singers. It is amusing to note that the ancients spoke of the melodious cow as standing for Taurus instead of the bull.

Taurus rules substance on all planes and all manner of possessions, from material to mental and spiritual. It is the universal storehouse, the Cosmic Womb of nature from whose substance all form finds birth. Taurus is naturally acquisitive, and these people have a feeling for possessions and making money. They have a dread of being destitute and are often bankers. "All that the Father has I Have, but I must earn it."

The keyword for Taurus is I HAVE. Their best quality is stability and their worst quality is stubbornness. In the less desirable expression Taurus can be utterly unmovable and headstrong, and can explode into a completely unexpected burst of temper when aroused.

Mercury has charge of the third sign, male Gemini. It is of air element and liquid in quality. Liquid air must go into the space reserved for it in your chart. Liquids are adaptable, being between gas and solids in density. Being of Mercury, the planet of expression, and of first degree emanation, the Gemini personality will express freely and often. Usually they have a great deal to say and enjoy saying it. Liquid air is just common air; it blows about in a natural way, heating or cooling according to the need. These folks are buoyant, full of ideas. You must go along with their ideas or be left behind. They are carefree, bounce up and down in their moods, try many things, and are never satisfied. Let them have full and free expression and they are seldom hard to get along with. The keyword for the air element is aspiration, and a Gemini is truly never satisfied, always asking for more, better possessions or higher ideals.

Gemini rules the shoulders, arms, hands and lungs. It is the sign of duality, for the incoming entity is a being of two worlds. Gemini is a thinker, using the outer or objective mind while its complementary sign, Sagittarius, is the inner or subjective mind. A Gemini is interested in many things. They are clever, often scientists, although sometimes they do not follow anything through to a conclusion but are off to another interest. They are restless, sensitive, intuitive, and interested in learning the why of things. It is called the child sign, possibly because of this very trait of asking questions.

The keyword for Gemini is I THINK. Their best quality is versatility and the worst is change-ability. In the less admirable expression a Gemini personality can be unstable, changeable, and switch from one idea to another with bewildering rapidity.

The Moon rules the fourth sign of the zodiac through female Cancer. It is gaseous water, which can best be compared with mist, not solid enough to be steam. They can be the most utterly un-happy people in the world one minute, but with a ray of sunshine in the form of a spoken word of sincere appreciation, they will respond and be as completely happy as they were completely un-happy. The Cancer people can be hurt very deeply but they never carry a grudge or harbor re-sentment. This is still first degree emanation, so the response is instantaneous, and they show their feelings. They are psychic, receptive, dreamy, and inclined to unexplained moods due to their highly receptive nature, which is attuned to the emotions and thoughts of those about them.

Cancer rules the breast, chest, stomach, and nourishing system of the body. It is the mother prin-ciple of Earth, as well as the people of Earth. This does not mean that the Moon is the mother of Earth. It is the mother principle, the nourishing principle, as the Moon affects all growing vege-tation. These people are domestic and also good business people, especially in real estate, food service, the hotel industry, and food handling and purveying. Cancer is the soul principle, whereby all experiences of life are received and recorded. The Cancer native is a born psychic and will sense intuitively what cannot be rationally explained. Awe and wonder are a part of Cancer characteristics, as is true humility. This humility is not a self-deprecation but a humility coming from an intuitive knowledge of man's helplessness without Divine guidance. All the water signs are psychic, but Cancer is the most psychic because it is the soul principle, and it is a function of the soul to receive and record all the experiences of that lifetime. Cancer people are not aggressive, but they are tenacious. A cat has claws and clings to what it has. So does a Can-cer person. The tenacity of a Cancer person matches the tenacity of the cat, which the ancients saw as the living symbol of Cancer. A Cancerian friend or mate will stick through thick and thin.

The keyword for Cancer is I FEEL. Their best quality is sensitivity and their worst quality is touchiness. In a less desirable expression of Cancer, the natives can be moody, reacting to the moods and emotions of others without knowing why.

Male Leo, the fifth sign, is under the rulership of the Sun. This is another fire sign, but solid fire this time. This can only be compared with a red-hot iron, which if it is to be handled at all must be allowed to cool off a bit and then handled with utmost diplomacy. This is the first of the sec-ond degree emanation signs and a comparison should be made between the freedom of Aries ex-pression and the expression of Leo, which is modified by mind. Although it is fire and therefore inspiration, it is not the direct inspiration of inner knowing, but rather is directed and influenced by mind and meditation. A red-hot iron can give off a friendly warmth on a cold day; Leo people are warm and friendly with a kindly interest. They will dominate you if allowed to do so, but they are convinced that they are doing so only for your own best good. They are concerned about you and are absolutely sure that they know what is best for you. Be prepared to be tactful if you oppose them.

Leo rules the heart, spine, diaphragm, and circulatory system, as well as the male organ of reproduction. It is the father principle and individuality expressing through the heart and soul and consciousness of self. It is the heart principle, humanity, and man. Leo is the playboy of the zodiac, the lover, although love affairs do not always bring happiness. They are not the workers. Seldom does a Leo enjoy manual work just for the sake of work. They may be involved the theater, drama, or dance, and will tell you that is work. Or they may direct activities, but they dislike manual work. They express the principle of young love, fun, drama, acting, dance, and all forms of entertainment.

The keyword for Leo is I WILL. The best quality is kindness and the worst is domination. In less admirable expression they can be dominant, the king and the lord of the manor.

Mercury rules the sixth sign, female Virgo. It is of the earth element and liquid in quality, as in the mortar that binds the bricks in a wall. A person who is responding correctly to Virgo vibrations will take all details, analyze them, and bind them to build a structure of facts. They are very much influenced by the mind, being of second degree emanation, and also Mercury, a mental planet.

Virgo is the master chemist, ruling the intestines. With Gemini, Virgo rules the breath, and with Pluto, rules the seed. Everything in life is born of a seed, immaculately conceived. Virgo is the keeper of the seed, the two half-seeds, the sperm and the ovum, before they are brought together by Libra, to form a complete seed in the womb of Taurus, through the process of union and conception. Virgo rules work, all kinds of work, but principally mental work. They are seldom the boss as they do not enjoy giving orders, but are often the power behind the throne, working hard to complete plans. Virgo, as the master chemist, also rules the work of the alimentary system of the body. Gemini takes in the food by way of the mouth (also thoughts and ideas to process), and Virgo makes it ready for use. In the small intestines the food is chemically changed into chyme and on into the building blocks for Mars the builder to use in building and repairing the human body. That which is not fit for use passes on into the colon for Scorpio to dispose of. Scorpio will find everything that is not right or of no use and dispose of it. The blood takes up what is usable for distribution all over the body, or Scorpio disposes of that which is not usable via the colon and the rectum. Libra disposes via the kidneys and pores.

Virgo is called the Virgin and the Harvest Maid, gathering all the experiences of life and enclosing them in a seed to be held safely until the next life calls them forth.

The keyword for Virgo is I ANALYZE. Their best quality is discrimination and their worst quality is criticism. In the less admirable expression, Virgo can analyze a thing until there isn't much left of your big dream. They can burst more bubbles just by being objective!

Venus rules the seventh sign, male Libra, which is of the air element and gaseous in quality—gaseous air. This reminds one of a merry summer breeze. Since Libra is by nature cheerful and happy, these are mild and pleasant, playful gusts of air. Libra is second degree emanation and not quite so free in expression as the air sign of first degree emanation, Gemini. They are easy people to get along with if you remember that they enjoy hearing nice things said about themselves, if said in sincerity. They also enjoy telling you all the nice things that they feel about you. Having everything harmonious in their surroundings is very important to Libra.

Libra rules the kidneys and the purification system, including the pores of the skin. It also rules partners, mates, marriage and mating, and the physical act of reproduction. Virgo's harvest of experiences are passed along in the seed to Libra for sowing. The growth of the seed brings forth the experiences of the next lifetime through the law that is known as the Law of Karma under Jupiter.

The keyword for Libra is I BALANCE. Their best quality is affection and their worst is love of flattery. When expressing in a less desirable way, there is a love of display and praise, an insatiable appetite for appreciation.

Mars rules the eighth sign of the zodiac, female Scorpio. It is of the water element and solid in quality. As solid water, the emotions are very much in evidence and are fixed and unchanging. These are the people who can hold a grudge and continue to hold on to a grievance. This is a misunderstood sign, so perhaps it is for this reason that it is hard to find a simile that really fits Scorpio. We immediately think of ice when we think of solid water, but that denotes a coldness that Scorpio does not necessarily have.

We have said that the Mars male sign, Aries, was the engineer of the system, managing everything from the top story, the head. And so they do, flying around, giving orders, and making plans before turning things over to the general manager, Scorpio, to carry out of the plans. Scorpio quietly manipulates matters until they have carried out their objective or have gotten their own way. And they do get their own way, even against Aries people, who seldom realize they have been managed. A Scorpio native is a good worker, but they do not take orders very well because they seldom need orders from another to carry out a project. If they meet an obstacle, they stick with it until they have it licked. In an argument they will not give up for the sake of peace, and lose respect for anyone who does. They can be a tower of strength to those who are confused or faltering.

Just as Aries rules the birth of form, Scorpio rules the death of form. It can only be the form (or body) of human life that ever dies, however, as spirit and soul merely separate from the physical form to allow them to return to the elements from which they came. Spirit and soul go on to another plane to await another form for more experiences of life on a higher spiral of evolution.

Scorpio rules the colon and the rectum; it is the garbage man of the human system, clearing away the debris of waste, the dead cells and the food waste, to leave the way clear for new construction. How could this possibly be a sex function? Yet present day astrologers persist in giving to Scorpio the sex function of human reproduction.

The keyword of Scorpio is I DESIRE. But the desire of Scorpio is not of a physical nature but a dynamic force of action. Without desire, nothing is accomplished. And it is the intense desire of Scorpio that paves the way for Mars to accomplish its purpose. Their best quality is resourcefulness and their worst is a troublesome fixation of purpose that will not give up long after others thought everything was settled. Somehow things turn out just the way Scorpio wants them to. Expression on a lower plane can take the form of jealousy, nursing a grievance, and holding onto a grudge long beyond the memory of the other person involved.

Jupiter rules male Sagittarius, the ninth sign of the zodiac. It is of the fire element, liquid in quality, and of third degree emanation, influenced by circumstances and environment. Liquid fire is best thought of as molten steel that can be molded into shape by pouring it into a mold. Or, in other words, will be molded by circumstances. Sagittarius has all the fire characteristics of Aries and Leo, but being of a different degree of emanation, those characteristics express in totally different ways. The keyword of the fire element is inspiration, coming from within.

Sagittarius also has an inner knowing, which is Jupiter's abstract law of nature, the universal mind or the mind that runs through all the manifested universe—nature—expressed through the principle of Jupiter, working through Sagittarius. It is the will of the Creator as Jupiter's law, the law of nature, and man on all planes. In man, Sagittarius is the subjective or mortal mind, not the spiritual mind, for that is the superconscious, or the mind of God, individualized in man. This can only be achieved by development and merging of all the functions of mind into a perfect expression of God mind.

In the human body Sagittarius rules the thighs, pelvic structure, loins, and groin. The keyword of Sagittarius is I SEE. The best quality is loyalty and the worst is deceit. Some authorities give sportiness as the lower expression of Sagittarius as many of the natives are very fond of sports, gambling, and physical pleasures.

Saturn rules female Capricorn, the tenth zodiacal sign. It is of earth element and gaseous in quality, or gaseous earth. This can best be thought of as dust. Capricorn is also of third degree emanation, responding to circumstances and environment. Capricorn represents the entry of the spirit monad (spirit entity) into matter as man was created (evolved) from the dust of Earth. Evolution depends on the crystallization principle of Saturn through the backward movement of Capricorn and the forward movement of Aquarius. In this it must be understood that the backward movement of Capricorn is not regression but a withdrawal to give impetus for the surge ahead. The whole process and purpose of evolution is the final perfection of man as the highest material expression of the Creator and man's preparation for work on the higher planes. The backward motion of Capricorn is evolution, the beginning of the return to spiritual Source. Spirit evolves the physical forms in which it functions. Each descent of spirit into matter is a backward motion preparatory to another forward motion into the realm of spirit.

Earth has practicality as its keyword. No amount of psychic ability would be of the slightest value without it being of practical use. Capricorn is the principle of use, of cooperation of all parts and coordinated functions. Capricorn natives can be misunderstood because of this very practicality, nevertheless they are often spiritual and usually psychic if they allow themselves to be. Of what benefit to humanity would psychic ability or spiritual knowledge be if it stayed mere theory, or kept hidden deep within as secret wisdom? It must be put to practical use if it is to benefit mankind.

Capricorn rules the knees and all joints in the human body, the skeleton and teeth. It rules big business, department stores, lumber and steel mills, and politics. Capricorn natives can be shrewd business people and politicians, but evolved Capricorns will turn their abilities to a higher plane. They all have ambition and a goal in life, which they strive to attain.

The keyword of Capricorn is I USE. Their best quality is diplomacy and their worst quality is trickiness.

Saturn also rules male Aquarius, the eleventh sign of the zodiac and of the air element and solid in quality—solid air. If you have ever tried to walk against a very strong wind and find that you cannot even go a single step, you will have an idea of just how solid air can be! The eye of a hurricane is an example; it is deathly still in the center, but one could not break out through the solid wall of air. The Aquarian native is like a whirlwind, so solid it is impossible to battle your way through it. It moves everything before it. It is of third degree emanation, and even though fixed in their beliefs, they are nevertheless sensitive to the thoughts and feelings of those around them, and influenced by environment. They are the humanitarians, the friends in need, interested in the whole of humanity. They are "winged" people with an elusive quality. Aquarius is the living electricity of the universe trying to be human and sometimes not fully stabilized; it is matter in abstract form. Aquarius is the vital, electric water of the universe, which becomes blood in man. It is the cosmic life force that flows through the solar system and our bodies. Leo (the complementary of Aquarius) rules the circulation of this force, the electromagnetic life to which Prana belongs. These people have an elusive quality, likened to the electric waves of cosmic electricity. They may be leaders of people, and are often diplomats. They usually set such high goals for themselves that they are never satisfied. They are progressive, ambitious, systematic, and love to argue. This sign rules all forward motion.

Aquarius rules the legs below the knees, ankles, calves, and shins. The keyword of Aquarius is I KNOW. But their knowing is of an inner knowing, not an educational knowledge. It is not of Mercury studies, so Aquarius could not be the exaltation of Mercury, as is often stated. Sometimes they are poor students, but they nevertheless have an intuitive knowing that they cannot always relate to reality. As ether is the essence of matter, so is this an unconscious intelligence within all substance; Aquarius brings it out from within to a gradual understanding. Their best quality is benevolence and their worst is a love of argument.

Jupiter rules the twelfth and last sign of the zodiac through female Pisces. This is a water sign and liquid in quality, so liquid water should not be hard to understand. Being of third degree emanation, Pisces natives are influenced by those around them and the circumstances of life in which they find themselves. Liquid water flows into all molds. They can be all things to all people. They are very adaptable and are found in all walks of life. They are very sympathetic to one in trouble, but are the least emotional of all the water signs. Pisces natives may be too much concerned with the problems of others for their own good, as they are prone to fear and worry for all mankind, but stable, dependable people.

Pisces rules law enforcement and karma, but karma must be understood to be correction for the growth of the individual, not punishment or reward. We sometimes hear the expression "weak as water," but what is weak about water? If you have ever watched a flood carry everything before it you will know that water is anything but weak. Nevertheless, the Pisces influence is not turbulent but quiet and free flowing like the depth of the ocean, exerting a tremendous strength of pressure. Scorpio is the stormy water on the top, Cancer the still waters that runneth deep, and Pisces the living waters that surround and protect the cell life of the body and the fetus within the body. All life has its start in water. Pisces rules that water and protects that life.

Pisces appears to have two opposite expressions: sympathy, kindliness and compassion, and strict law enforcement! Pisces rules prisons for those who break laws, as well as hospitals where we are sometimes imprisoned for our own good when we have broken the laws of health. But Pisces only imprisons for a purpose. The laws of Jupiter have to be enforced, and this is the function of Pisces. Even the broken moral laws, which our man-made laws cannot reach, come under the rulership of Pisces. They are those we call karma that we can never evade no matter how hard we may try.

The Pisces function rules faith—the faith in Jupiter's laws that governs all things in the manifested universe. It rules religion and philosophy. If these individuals are not very highly evolved, it is possible for them to become fanatics because they believe what they believe with their whole hearts. It is an unquestioning acceptance relative to the Piscean Age from which we are just now emerging. We were told to believe, to have faith; that was all that was ever needed. Using our own God-given minds to seek higher knowledge was frowned upon.

Pisces rules the feet in the human body, the magnetic point of contact with Mother Earth. The keyword of Pisces is I BELIEVE. Their best quality is sympathy and their worst is worry.

The symbology of the signs follows the same pattern as that of the planets inasmuch as they tell a story about the nature of the sign.

Aries is represented by the ram (or the lamb) and its symbol indicates the horns of the ram. The ancients recognized that sometimes an Aries native was more to be likened to a lamb than to the head-on impulsiveness of the ram. The basic characteristics are still there, but of a gentler expression. So keep in mind that they used both the ram and the lamb as the living symbols for Aries. The horns are turned down as though encasing the whole, managing the whole system.

Taurus is represented by the cow, and its symbol indicates the round face that a Taurus native often has, with the horns of the cow pointing upward as if indicating that all substance comes from on high, the horn of plenty upturned to receive.

Gemini, the twins, represents duality, indicated by the two upright lines, as two upward-reaching arms, with the curved, upreaching line across the top indicative of the reaching outward and upward, the restless search of Gemini for more, or better possessions or bigger and better ideals, but with a solid base.

Cancer, the mother principle, represents the two arms across the bosom, cradling the babe to the breast, and the nourishing, protective principle of motherhood—the Everlasting Arms, the Mother principle of Deity.

Leo, the father principle, is the male reproductive organ, the phallus in an upright position and the sac containing the sperm. "The organ in which God dwells," and held sacred by the ancients as being the only organ capable of bringing human life into existence. The Father principle of Deity.

Virgo, the Virgin, is the keeper of the virgin seed or the Harvest Maid with a sheaf of wheat tied around with a loop. This is also representative of the loop of the intestine, which Virgo rules.

Libra's symbol represents the scales, balance, the equilibrium to be maintained between spirit and matter.

Scorpio, with its arrow pointing downward, has a significance all its own. This pertains to its purely physical function of elimination, downward and out, via the rectum. It is not the sting of the scorpion. In the world of ancient astrology, the eagle, not the scorpion, was the living symbol for Scorpio. For the eagle, the arrow was pointed upward, depicting the soul in its upward flight after leaving the body at death.

Sagittarius the Centaur is half-man and half-animal, or half-human mind and half-animal or instinctive mind, with a small line dividing it in two segments. The arrow pointing upward symbolizes the mind winging its way toward the height, seeking its highest expression.

If the symbol for Capricorn ever had a particular significance, it has been lost in time or changed to such a degree that it is no longer recognizable. The goat, as the living symbol for Capricorn, is the one animal with the sure instinct for climbing higher. The rocky path they follow is but a stepping stone for their ambitious plans.

The symbol for Aquarius is pictured as the waves of etheric energy or the living electricity of the universe. It is pictured as a person with an urn pouring water upon the ground, but actually means the universal man pouring out upon the earth the living waters (etheric energy) of the universe.

Pisces, the fishes, represents the two parts of the mind turned in opposite directions but forever joined until the time when they will turn toward each other and become completely merged. It is two expressions of one mind, one turning outward toward life and its duties, the other turning inward to the higher self; the inner mind is always striving toward spirit. They are looking in opposite directions but tied together, indicating that we can never get away from that part of us which is Divine Essence.

As a reminder, every sign reflects the nature of the principle (the planet) that functions through it. The force and energy of Mars is reflected in impetuous Aries and determined Scorpio. Aries gives the orders, Scorpio does the work. Once the exaltation, as the highest expression of a planet, is understood, it is easy to understand the fall. It can readily be seen that Mars, for example, with its impetuous nature could not possibly express true to its nature through its fall, Cancer. Cancer is dreamy, domestic, receptive. There is no likeness to Mars in any way. This is also true with the detriments; social Libra or timid Taurus, both Venus signs, could not possibly express the nature of Mars. When Mars is at home in Aries or Scorpio, it can express freely according to its nature, but when in the home of Venus it modifies its expression according to the nature of Venus.

Everything in the chart is modified by all the other principles. Every planet, sign, house, and aspect modifies and changes the total picture. The sign the Sun occupies at birth is considered your birth sign and denotes your deep, inner, and often hidden individuality, what you are deep inside. This may not show to a casual observer, or even to someone who is well acquainted with you. The outer self, the personality, is shown by the rising sign, or the Ascendant, which indicates appearance as well as personality. The personality may be in harmony with the individuality, or it may be in complete inharmony. This can only be determined by a study of the nature of the two signs and their ruling planets. The Sun sign may be dynamic, positive, and forceful, while the rising sign is gentle and retiring. Then we have a person who is in conflict with himself or herself. If the Sun and rising signs are the same, the person has "no mask to hide behind."

Summary
1. The zodiacal signs are of our solar system alone; the orb of their influence is within our own boundaries and has no affect outside our solar system.

2. When viewed from any point on Earth, the orbits of all the planets are an apparent motion only.

3. The twelve signs are classed in various ways, all descriptive of their nature; two groups of six signs each specify the sex; four groups of three signs each designate the element; three groups of four signs each are classed as to quality; and four groups of three signs each in sequence show the degree of emanation.

4. The keyword for each sign also tells you something of its nature, as well as the animal or other object chosen to represent it.

5. There are ten planets, twelve signs, twelve houses, and innumerable aspects, making your chart individually yours. So do not attempt to judge yourself by your sun sign; everything in the chart influences and modifies or strengthens it.

6. The signs alone do not indicate ability as much as they indicate potential. If we develop the potential we express the highest nature of the sign and our talents and abilities are strengthened and available for our use.

7. The pattern of the planets in the sky at birth corresponds to the soul-pattern of the individual for this lifetime. It is a working pattern, not a pattern of our evolutionary status. That is shown only by the way we react to the experiences of life.

8. Planetary vibrations strike our inner being, the centers within us which correspond to them and work outward. We attract events into our lives by the way we respond to that vibration.

CHAPTER 8

THE HOUSES AND THE ASPECTS

It would be incomplete to bring any discourse on astrology to a close without saying a few words about the houses and the aspects, although good and useful information, and in greater detail than we can go into here, can be found in any good book on astrology.

The houses are divisions of the energy field of the Earth and pertain to Earth alone. The houses map the experiences we are to have in this lifetime, the work we will have to do. These experiences are not thrown at us from the planets however. They come to us from within ourselves, a direct result of how we have met past experiences, how we have lived past lives, what karma—good or bad—we have laid up for ourselves. They show us our unpaid debts thereby giving us an opportunity to pay them, ridding ourselves of their unwelcome influence in our lives. These debts we bring with us into each lifetime via the life seed. Each must be paid in full and the opportunity for this is shown by the houses in our personal natal chart.

There are valuable lessons to be had from the experiences of life. Whether we learn that lesson or rebel against it is up to us. In this we have free will. The way we react, the thoughts we have in connection with it, attract other events into our lives either fortunate or unfortunate. There definitely is a magnetic attraction to our thought. We have all seen people who seem to attract misfortune and others who seem to lead a charmed life. While the houses map the karmic condition we are living now, the thoughts and actions we employ in dealing with them determine the karmic condition of the future, both in this life and in future ones. Love is the most powerful attractive force in the world, but fear also attracts. If our lives are governed by an abnormal fear of some disease for instance, we are pretty apt to attract that disease to us in later life.

Thoughts of hope, happiness and good fortune bring good fortune to us through the power of magnetic attraction. Although it is a known fact that like attracts unlike and negative attracts positive in the realm of matter; in the mental realm, like attracts like. So when something happens in our lives, some misfortune or grief, know that it is one of the lessons of life and an opportunity to grow. Rise above it and you have overcome to a powerful degree your weaker, mortal self. This is one of the most valuable of the lessons to be learned in a correct understanding of astrology and of the houses that map our experiences in life, those events we cannot evade.

People often say they do not believe in astrology because they do not believe that the planets have an influence over their lives; they want to rule the planets! Well, free will is a priceless possession, but it does not include an ability to rule the heavenly bodies. It merely gives us an opportunity to rule our own reactions to these influences. It gives us an opportunity to cooperate with that force instead of opposing it.

Every house maps the karma in our lives, that which we brought in with us. Every house has the influence of the sign on the cusp and the planet that rules that sign, as well as the natural ruler of the house and its ruling planet. For example, Mars rules the first house in the natural chart. If your rising sign is Virgo, then Mercury rules your first house and determines your personality and appearance; but the influence of Aries and Mars is still a secondary influence.

The houses revolve with the Earth, and a different sign appears over the eastern horizon every two hours, a different degree of that sign every four minutes. The planet posited in any house maps the experiences we will have in the department designated by the house and according to the nature of the planet, modified, strengthened, or weakened by the sign it is in.

The first house denotes birth, the nature of the personality, and the appearance. The personality is the outer self, that which is first noted when meeting a person for the first time, and often the only part of the individual we ever really see. The sign that the Sun occupies contains the unseen unexpected qualities, the inner being. These two may be at variance with each other and this will show up as conflict within the person to whom the chart belongs.

The second house shows our possessions, that which we value, and indicates if these possessions are of a material, mental, or spiritual nature.

The third house is the house of childhood, our relatives (especially siblings), our neighbors, all that is close to us in childhood. It is also our childhood studies, short journeys of the mind as well as actual voyages.

The fourth house is the home, one parent, usually the father. In this house are found all the things connected with the home: real estate, hotels (home away from home), and since Cancer is the natural ruler of the fourth house and is the nourishing principle, it rules food markets, health stores, restaurants and any business pertaining to the handling of food.

The fifth house corresponds to the teen years, young love, all affairs of the heart, fun, entertainment, drama, love, all affairs of the heart, fun, entertainment, drama, the dance, and the theater. The lesson to be learned in this house is that real happiness does not come from without but must come from within ourselves. This house is also our children and our own youth, and the house of speculation and the stock market.

The sixth house is the experiences we will have in work and service, our health or sickness. It rules our servants, the trades, and chemistry, especially food chemistry.

The seventh house is the experience of balance in our relationships, especially the marriage partner but also people in general. It shows us our out-in-the-open enemies. It also rules the element of war—cooperate or do battle. There must be cooperation in marriage or it may end in a battle in a divorce court.

The eighth house is the house of other peoples' money—wages, inheritance, and public funds. This is the house of the change called death, for death is but a change of condition or form. The astral world is represented by the eighth house.

The ninth house represents our experiences in advanced studies and the professions, especially law, philosophy, and religion. It rules universities, advertising, and publishing.

The tenth house rules our ambitions in life and its final achievement. Big business, status, and the boss all come under the tenth house. Here we find the influence of the other parent, the one with the most influence in our lives, usually the mother.

The eleventh house shows the experiences we will have with friends and associates, our hopes and wishes. When this house is occupied by many planets or is heavily aspected, the individual is apt to care more for friends and companions than for family.

The twelfth house maps experiences with hospitals, prisons, and law enforcement agencies. Any place of confinement with or without our consent is indicated by the twelfth house. It shows the secret enemies or forces that work against us. All the houses map our karma, but this house shows us what the others do not show: our limitations, frustrations, disappointments, sorrows, and self-undoing (which does not mean suicide), and all the ways in which we retard our own progress.

The planets we find in these houses do not rule them; rather, they maps the nature of the experiences we will have in that department of life. You will notice that each house has at least two different functions, related in nature but different. We must be alert to determine which of the two is indicated in any particular chart. In the eighth house, for example, does it focus on handling public funds or is the experience to be of a psychic nature in the astral realm? In the tenth house, does the experience relate to active business participation or is it the strong influence of the mother? All things must be carefully considered: the influence of the sign governing that house in the natural chart and its ruling planet, the sign on the cusp and its ruling planet, any planet that may be in the house and the sign that it is functioning through, and lastly, but very important, the aspects between the planets.

Before we study the aspects, however, it's important to know that the houses that are opposite each other in the chart have similar functions. For instance, the third house governs childhood studies and the ninth house governs advanced studies and higher education; the tenth has to do with one parent, and the fourth house with the other. The first house in self, and the seventh is the mate

The tenth house is the strongest house in the chart. Any planet posited there has a stronger influence than if it were in any other house. The first house is the next in strength, then the fourth, and the seventh. These are known as the angular houses. Each is ruled by a cardinal sign (in the natural chart) and each stands at one of the four compass points. The succedent houses, or those that succeed the angular, have the next greatest strength and are, by the degree of their influence, the eleventh, the second, the eighth, and the fifth. The cadent houses have the mildest influence and are, by the degree of their strength, the twelfth, the third, the ninth, and the sixth.

The aspects show us the nature of the experiences we are to have in this lifetime, whether they will be hard, with obstacles and frustrations, or easygoing. Each aspect serves as a stimulus or depressant upon which the growth of the soul depends. They strengthen or inhibit the work of the planets in relation to each other.

The square is known as an obstacle aspect, and here we will find obstacles to our progress and the things that we hope to accomplish relative to the work mapped by the house and the nature of the planets involved. They are not insurmountable obstacles, but they certainly offer a challenge. A chart with many squares is considered a difficult chart, but it is interesting to note that most of the famous people of history, both men and women, have many squares in their charts, thus having to contend with frustrations and adverse circumstances. Those who do have many squares are usually worthwhile, progressive people. But it is still the individual behind the chart that determines whether the life will be a good and useful one or that of wasted opportunities.

As an example, a resistor slows the flow of electricity through a wire much as water would be slowed if it were diverted into a smaller hose, thus causing more pressure, which in turn would produce more force and power. The resistor holds back the free-flowing electricity, thereby causing more power to be generated. This is exactly what happens in our own lives when we set about quietly and with control, drawing upon the spiritual strength within us, to solve the problems mapped by the square. We develop a spiritual power within us that we would be unlikely to achieve if we had no particular problems to overcome. The lesson to be learned from the square is for us to develop our inner strength by drawing upon the God-given power within us.

People rejoice when they find many trine aspects in their charts, but a life replete with luck may very easily become a life becalmed, an easy life, and consequently they seldom develop their inner strength. These fortunate aspects are a result of former achievements, but we cannot coast along on former glory. This life, too, must be one of advancement, a productive life, if we hope to better ourselves. The lesson to be learned from the trine is to exert our capabilities to the fullest, not only for ourselves but to be of help to others. We must use force and initiative. Those with many trines may become lazy, something that must be guarded against. Things come too easily and these individuals do not need to exert themselves. They are contented and nice to be around, but tend to depend too much on luck.

With the opposition, the force of the vibrations meet head-on. It is called the separation aspect and generally considered to be a hard one. However, as in most other conditions, we find that we have a choice, and the results depend upon the use we have made of an opportunity. We can meet conditions head-on and battle it out. Or we can ease past, gradually and gently, cooperating instead of opposing. It may be likened to a hand-shake as the two people involved are stationed directly opposite each other, but they are not opposing each other. So it is with the planets involved in this aspect. Their forces are meeting head-on, but those forces can be managed to be of mutual help and strength. The Moon is directly opposite the Sun at the time of the Full Moon. From this position it receives its greatest illumination, with the full glory reflected in all its beauty. The lesson to be learned from the opposition is cooperation, not opposition.

The conjunction is known as the power aspect because each planet lends power to and strengthens the other. Where many conjunctions are found in a chart the individual may appear so sure as to arouse resentment in others. Nevertheless it indicates strength and a powerful personality. The lesson to be learned here is to use discrimination, to know when to stop. These people may have their eyes so firmly fixed upon the future and their objectives that they may not realize how this affects others. Moderation and discrimination must be learned and used.

The sextile is the opportunity aspect. Here the planets are harmonious and bring unexpected opportunities to the individual. However, the time of influence is shorter so often the opportunity comes and goes before it is recognized. The lesson to be learned here is to be ever-alert and watchful. If there are many sextiles in a chart it shows a life replete with opportunities, but the individual must be alert so that they do not vanish before they are recognized.

The semisquare is the friction aspect, a source of irritation. The lesson is one of patience and endurance, which when learned, result in poise and harmony. The semisquare represents things we would like to get rid of but cannot shake. However, the time element is relatively short and the knowledge that "this too will pass" if we have patience will help us to endure.

The sesquisquare is the agitation aspect and maps the things in life that we really want and seldom get, those things that we try in vain to attain. It is an illusive promise and seldom fails to disappoint us. The lesson here is detachment. If we try with all our might to attain something and still fail, then release it completely from your mind, knowing that it is beyond reach and that no good will come from holding it in your thoughts.

The semisextile is the growth aspect. Here too we must learn cooperation, and although it will work to our benefit, we must also work. We cannot sit back and wait for something to happen. We have to nourish it through our thoughts and our actions.

The inconjunct aspect is one of over-optimism. We are as inclined to use poor judgment and moderation as we are apt to attempt things beyond our ability to achieve. Many inconjunctions in a chart denote an insecure person, rather other-worldly and vague. The influences from this aspect may prompt people to make special preparations for big events that somehow fail to materialize. The inconjunct is like a mirage.

Each of the aspects is similar in nature to one of the planets:

Conjunction: Sun
Semisextile: Moon
Semisquare: Mercury
Sextile: Venus
Square: Mars
Trine: Jupiter
Sesquisquare: Uranus
Inconjunct: Neptune
Opposition: Saturn

Always consider the harmony or inharmony of all factors—planet, sign, house, and aspect. There are no hard and fast rules to be followed in determining if a really unfortunate event is in store for us, but it is generally conceded that harmonious planets and signs are beneficial even if they form a square or other so-called discordant aspects. And of course, we do keep in mind that these less desirable aspects are not disasters but are to be considered as a challenge.

A working knowledge of astrology as a whole, with an understanding of the aspects, makes it possible for us to confront our problems in an intelligent and understanding way, thereby finding a solution for them. It will be of help in understanding our mates and children, our friends and associates, and most important of all, ourselves. It will prevent our demanding more from them than they are able to produce, and help us to recognize and develop latent talents.

Summary
1. All of the factors in a chart are important and must be considered in relation to all other factors.

2. Houses denote the departments of life in which we have experiences, learn lessons, and work out karma, or pay debts to further our progress.

3. A planet indicates the kind of experiences we will have relative to the nature of the planet as modified by the sign it occupies.

4. The aspects are tools for our use and show us where we will encounter help or hindrances.

5. We have forged these aspects (experiences) ourselves, and are now forging aspects for future lives.

6. All our lives consist of a variety of lessons; we cannot escape them.

7. These lessons can be used as stepping stones to rise to a higher plane of life.

CHAPTER 9

SOME AFTERTHOUGHTS

Now I find that I have reached the end of the message that I have been entrusted to pass along to those who are still seeking answers to questions that continue to puzzle. I wish to repeat that this effort to restate ancient concepts of astrology can only be considered in the light of a mere beginning. I hope it will stimulate other minds to continue the search, to gather up the loose ends, and to continue to weave the pattern that my teacher began so long ago. My own life has taken on a whole new dimension, vastly enriched because of the knowledge passed on to me by my teacher. However for every answer that we have found there are many questions that remain unanswered. Those answers are somewhere. With all my heart, I hope this message will inspire others to join our search.

I could fill pages with as yet unanswered questions. A few of the more vexing (vexing because I feel the answers are at hand but I have failed to grasp them) are: Does the symbol for Pisces also suggest the soul-mates, two half-beings separated in this Earth life, yet forever united by a magnetic tie? Through the ages of time will they be united again in a perfect, composite, spiritual being, a whole personality once again, after the lessons of the flesh have been mastered, as they were before the "fall" into materiality before the Adamic period?

For how many lifetimes am I to be a Virgo? Will I always belong to the same planetary family, lifetime after lifetime? Or after I have perfected myself in the experiences that Mercury has to offer do I then start another series of experiences through another planetary family? If so, will it be Jupiter, the other planet of the mental plane, under Neptune? Occult tradition tells us that we inhabit both the male and the female body in successive lives in order to complete our experiences and the lessons to be gained thereby. So be it, but will I always be either a Virgo or a Gemini, of the planetary family of Mercury? There are many theories, and I have a few of my own, but is there an authoritative source where I can get a reasonably logical answer?

When and why were the living symbols for the signs of the zodiac changed? Why did the scorpion replace the eagle? The crab replace the cat? The astrological scorpion and crab are not mentioned in the Kabala or the Bible. The symbol for death (Scorpio) is the eagle. The eagle's upward flight into the sun symbolizes the soul's upward flight as it leaves the physical body. Why did the bull become the living symbol for Taurus instead of the cow? Why was Libra, the sign of male and female union, removed from the zodiac for a period of time? We believe it could only have come about at the time of phallic worship.

Why do present-day astrologers persist in saying that Scorpio is a sex sign when the very nature of our anatomy renders it impossible? This too must have come from decadent times, down through the Dark Ages, and has remained with us only because it has been unchallenged. In our more enlightened knowledge of astrology, we have no use for remnants left over from the days of phallic worship.

This will give us some idea of the momentous work that lies ahead. I find myself unable to cease my constant searching for the answers to questions that remain unsolved. It is a fascinating and enriching experience.

The ten planets and the twelve zodiacal signs correspond to the twenty-two spiritual and cosmic principles of the sacred teaching. The Hebrew alphabet is based upon these twenty-two sacred principles, yet it continues to puzzle our astrologers because there are only ten planets when there are twelve signs and they continue to look for two more planets. Only an understanding of the secondary suns can satisfactorily explain it when used together with an understanding of the polarity of the signs through which the planets function.

The many changes that have taken place in man's understanding—or rather, misunderstanding—and beliefs concerning astrology can have no effect other than the natural confusion resulting from it. It would make no difference whatever to the cosmic what we think. We cannot change a cosmic decree nor declare a cosmic law. Would the Ruler of the heavens be aware that we had made these weighty decisions? The age-old laws of the universe would still be in effect just as though little man had never spoken. Our only hope is to continue to seek the truth. Somewhere, sometime, more of this ancient hidden Truth will be revealed.

The twenty-two cards of the tarot correspond completely to the twenty-two sacred principles of ancient scriptures, which in turn correspond to the ten planets and the twelve signs. They contain the inner meaning, the spiritual interpretation of astrology. Forty cards called the Minor Arcana have been added, making a total of seventy-eight cards. These later additions have no value at all to astrology. They merely make the art of fortune-telling more interesting and were added for that purpose.

I realize that at times in this work the switch from concrete facts to abstractions and back again has been confusing, but the line between the two worlds is very thin. It is non-existent except in man's own mortal concept. Truth itself is an abstraction, and is available to each of us at all times from the Central Source. We block the way for the free-flowing tide through our preconceived conclusions that may have no basis whatsoever in fact. Everything of the material world is controlled and directed by abstract principle. It could be no other way.

So many times in our own lives we have found that a complete explanation of a problem presented its own solution. Knowledge can be had by all who care to pursue it, but knowledge, like food, has to go through a digestive process before it can be of the slightest use to us. It must become a part of our consciousness. We can learn to combine the objective, logical, reasoning process of Mercury with the subjective process of Jupiter, meditating upon our accumulated knowledge until the abstract principles are made clear, thus is true wisdom gained. This wisdom can be shared and still remain our own. Knowledge is of the objective, concrete world, subject to time and change. Wisdom belongs to the ages, both past and future. It becomes a beacon light guiding us on our chosen path. It is a satisfying, inspiring, exciting, and rewarding path. I hope you will find new adventures along the paths and by-paths and discover for yourself how astrology relates to other sciences and all religious beliefs.

If you are tempted to discard the concepts set forth on these pages, first ask yourself if you are retaining a principle in which you sincerely believe and are convinced is a true concept. Or are you defending a prejudice because it is one that has been generally accepted up to the present time.

The mark of a really individualized person is the ability to stand alone, to think individually, to remain uninfluenced by the thought vibrations of the group, of society as a whole. It is a true indication of one's stature, and usually the mark of a lonely soul.

I take no credit for my teacher's work. She spent nearly fifty years of her life in concentrated effort and constant search to assemble the facts I have presented in these pages. It is my deep regret that she has chosen to remain anonymous, requesting simply that these concepts go forth to benefit humanity. There will be many, however, who will recognize her teachings, many who were former students of hers, and they will know to whom to give credit. Nearly all of this book was read and approved by her discriminating eye, or read and disapproved, and so rewritten until it met with her approval before she passed on to a higher realm of life. Mine has been a labor of love and gratitude for her patient teaching.

In closing I can find no better words that those used by Helena Blavatsky, from an old Hindu philosopher: "Never utter these words 'I do not know this, therefore it is false.' One must study to know, know to understand, and understand to judge."

www.ingramcontent.com/pod-product-compliance
Lightning Source LLC
LaVergne TN
LVHW081325060426
835511LV00011B/1862